"As he thinks in his heart, so is he"

YOUR THOUGHTS SHAPE YOUR LIFE

Unlocking the power of positive thinking from a Christian perspective

Published by Terry J. Boyle
Copyright © Terry John Boyle 2026.

Unless otherwise noted, all scripture quotations are taken from the Holy Bible, New King James Version Copyright © 1979, 1980, 1982 by Thomas Nelson, Inc.

All rights reserved. No part of this book may be reproduced in any form, stored in a retrieval system, or transmitted in any form by any means—electronic, mechanical, photocopy, recording or otherwise—without the prior written permission of the publisher, except as provided by Australian copyright law.

Words in capitals, or in bold or italics are the emphases of the author Terry Boyle – terryjohnboyle@bigpond.com

Cover & typeset by Carl Butel at Deep Image – carl@deepimage.net.au

Cataloguing-in-Publication data is available from the National Library of Australia.

ISBN 978-1-7642408-1-9
eBook ISBN 978-1-7642408-2-6

Acknowledgments

I thank my wife, Caroline, for her love, support, and encouragement. Additionally, I would like to thank our children —Amanda, Felicity, Andrew, and Sharon —and their spouses and children for their unwavering support.

Special thanks to our daughter, Amanda, for her input and encouragement, and to her husband, Carl Butel, for his brilliant cover design and layout, which made the presentation ready for printing.

I thank my son, Andrew, a Baptist minister, for his editorial work, input, wise suggestions, and doctrinal insight.

I thank the Rev. Rod Dymock, my associate pastor for 21 years in Lismore, for his foreword to this book and for his encouragement and input into my life over many years. I also thank the leaders of various denominations for their fellowship and input, as well as my long-standing association with A2A. Thanks to those at Life Ministry Church in Melbourne, those on the Mission Field in Papua New Guinea, those at Centre Church in Lismore, NSW, Australia, and those we currently fellowship with on the Gold Coast.

CONTENTS

Foreword

Introduction

1. An explanation of the context
2. The past is gone; the future is yours
3. You may not be as perfect as you think
4. God can do more than you imagine
5. The way you think affects your attitude
6. Your mind is not renewed overnight
7. You can overcome negative thoughts
8. A good report will impact many lives
9. You can be strong and courageous
10. Be graciously optimistic about the future
11. Your vision must have a purpose
12. Be inspired by Godly affirmations
13. Do not neglect the marginalised
14. Avoid going into panic mode
15. Go after the life you are hoping for
16. Speak positively, or stay silent
17. You need to recharge your spirit
18. Joyful faith, fun, and fellowship
19. Take time to think outside the box
20. Are you thinking beyond the grave?

Foreword

The timeless truths of the Bible, when studied, meditated on, digested and assimilated into daily life, produce personal transformation and successful Christian living. One such truth—"How your thoughts shape your life"—through the power of biblical faith thinking is what Rev. Terry Boyle puts under the microscope in his latest book. He clearly and capably shows how to apply this scriptural truth in life and in Christian ministry.

Terry writes from decades of dedicated ministry and mission, and hence, authentic wisdom resounds through the pages of this readable book, so rich in insights and illustrations hammered on the anvil of faith experiences.

It is a personal honour for me to write this foreword, as I have travelled the ministry road with Terry for over 20 years: as his associate minister and as Principal of the Christian school the church had pioneered and of which he was board chair.

So many picturesque memories come to mind as I reflect on those many years of serving together in ministry and leadership. Terry was an inspirational and considerate boss as well as a wonderful colleague and friend, along with his wife, Caroline and their family. I have seen first-hand his diligent application of the scriptural principles he teaches in these writings.

The central truth he so thoroughly addresses is a shining gemstone from the Bible, and Terry captures many facets of this principle that daily reflect the goodness of God in human experience.

Throughout the chapters, Terry keeps the discourse moving and enriches it with illustrations, testimonies, and humour. This book is also richly soaked in scripture from which the reader, open to the Spirit, will gain much spiritual illumination and inspiration along the way.

I happily recommend this literary work by Terry Boyle as pleasantly readable and practical, yet profoundly enlightening and transformative. As you read, reflect and apply these truths, you may encounter Jesus in a new way through these pages.

Rev. Rod Dymock *B.E. (Elec Hon) B. Min.*

Former Senior Pastor, Centre Church, Lismore, N.S.W. and former Principal of Summerland Christian College.

Introduction

This is my eighth book, and probably the most challenging one for me. The biggest battles I have faced as a pastor and missionary have not been so much about external circumstances and achievements as about internal conflicts related to what is commonly called the battle of the mind.

My greatest struggle has been shifting from a negative to a positive mindset. I have had to focus on what I dwell on, meditate on, and believe in. I have realised how much our thoughts matter to God and how they also have a powerful effect on us, shaping our lives.

"As a man thinks in his heart, so is he" (Proverbs 23:7). Although this is taken out of context (which I will explain later) to use as a scripture to promote positive thinking, it is still an essential principle and a truth that is supported by other scriptures. What we think in our hearts about ourselves will not only shape our lives, but also those we live with, fellowship with, and minister to. Our thoughts are the unseen force that influences our decisions, our words, and our actions. They shape our identity and our destiny.

Many years ago, Norman Vincent Peale wrote a great book called The Power of Positive Thinking. To put it his way,

Introduction

"You are not what you think you are, but you are – what you think." It was a highly successful book and had a profound impact on both Christians and non-Christians.

Why then did I bother to write this book? I felt led to write it because I have discovered that many books on the power of positive thinking are written in a "disconnected from God format." They seem more dependent on self-effort and mental gymnastics, with a new-age flavour—but positive thinking is far more than mind over matter. Some of these books have nothing to do with what is in our hearts, how we connect with God, or how we apply His word to our lives.

All of us, to varying degrees, carry emotional and psychological wounds from our past that affect the way we think, speak, and act. Some of us will succumb to our past and become a victim of soul-destroying thoughts of guilt and shame, and write ourselves off as failures, with a negative outlook on life. However, it is possible to be transformed by the renewing of our minds, which enables us to overcome our flaws and fears, so that we might accomplish great things in the name of the Lord. "… the people who know their God shall be strong and do great exploits." Daniel 11:22.

From a theological perspective, I have discussed these complex issues with several ministerial friends, who encouraged me to write a book on positive thinking from a balanced Christian viewpoint.

In this book, I will take you on a spiritual journey that can transform your life and help you address essential questions.

Are your thoughts shaping your life by building you up or breaking you down? Is your thinking limiting your potential, or is it releasing your faith to make your dreams a reality?

Throughout this book, I will share Word-based principles from my life and ministry experiences to help you on this life-changing journey.

Chapter 1

An explanation of the context

Some years ago, in a 60 Minutes television interview, Pauline Hanson, an Australian politician, was asked by host Tracey Curro if she was xenophobic, to which Hanson replied, "Please explain."

Following the interview, "Please explain" became a well-used quote, initially to ridicule politicians or anyone else who naively needed to have something explained to them. I felt this was somewhat unfair. In case you are wondering, xenophobia, according to the Oxford Dictionary, means a morbid dislike of foreigners.

When I was sharing thoughts for this book with someone, they asked me to "Please explain" the original context of *"as a man thinks in his heart, so is he"* (Proverbs 23:7). So, I will now explain the context for you before using it as our primary text.

It is easy to take something out of context and use it to prove a point. However, it should also be explained in the original context for which it was intended. This verse is widely accepted and used to promote positive thinking, even though it may differ from its original meaning. We will explore later how numerous other scriptures support the application of this scripture to our thought process.

To understand the context, we need to consider the surrounding verses. *"Do not eat the bread of a miser, nor desire his delicacies; for as he thinks in his heart, so is he. "Eat and drink!" he says to you, but his heart is not with you. The morsel you have eaten, you will vomit up, and waste your pleasant words."* Proverbs 23:6-8.

The context reveals this phrase, "But his heart is not with you." What does this mean from a practical and spiritual perspective? It cautions against associating with individuals who are deceptive, stingy, or insincere, even if they appear generous and sincere. However, their true nature is often hidden in their hearts.

They may invite you to eat and drink with them and be polite to your face, but their character is hidden; they have ulterior motives, and their heart is not with you. Their inner thoughts and actions do not align with their verbal thoughts. So, what he thinks in his heart is what the real person is like… "So is he."

Human nature has not changed. *"Help, Lord, for the godly are no more; the faithful have vanished from among men. Everyone lies to his neighbour; their flattering lips speak with deception."* Psalm 12:1-2.

Although written over two thousand years ago, its message remains timeless and resonates with us today.

The issues of life stem from the heart

The everyday issues of life — our thoughts, actions, and what we ultimately do — stem from the condition of our hearts. *"Keep your heart with all diligence, for out of it spring the issues of life."* Proverbs 4:22-23.

To keep your heart with all diligence means to watch over what influences and shapes your inner feelings and thoughts, for everything in life flows out of the heart. Our words and actions shape what we say and do.

We live in a world that is often dishonest and deceptive; therefore, it is essential to be open, honest, and positive at the same time. We should not try to hide anything; instead, we should think before we speak and choose our words wisely.

I knew a doctor who, through his oversized glasses, had a penetrating stare, as though he was looking into your heart. He would glare at you and say, "How are you really going?" Then, he would wait with a prolonged silence. It was as if he suspected you were hiding something, and you had better tell him everything and not try to conceal anything. We cannot — and should not—hide anything from God; He knows what is in our hearts. The problem we face is knowing what is in someone else's heart, so we are not being deceived.

Jesus also warns us of increasing deception and betrayal in the last days (Matthew 24). At some stage, we have probably all been deceived and betrayed in what we thought was a good deal or a good relationship. However, the implication is that deception will become more prevalent in the last days and that we should hopefully be able to discern it.

Having explained the context of "As a man thinks in his heart, so is he." Throughout this book, we will explore how, from a Christian perspective, our thoughts regarding the power of positive thinking can shape our lives.

Chapter 2

The past is gone; the future is yours

"Do not think about the past. Look at the new things I am going to do. It is already happening. Don't you see it?"

Isaiah 43:18-19 NCV.

We need to stop looking back to what we were and start seeing ourselves as who we are in Christ. As Christians, our past is gone; it has been crucified with Christ. The future is ours, but some worldly memories still linger on to haunt us. This is one of the reasons we need to take action and renew our minds.

There is no shortage of our desire to seek a better future. Most of us desire to be successful and somehow make a difference. We may desire to lose weight, but what are we going to do about it? The problem is a lack of action. Sometimes, it seems there is a vast distance between our desires and our actions. We use the expression *"You need to put feet on your faith"* based on scriptures like, *"Faith by itself, if it does not have works (actions) is dead"… "Show me your faith without your works (actions), and I will show you my faith by my works (actions)."* James 2:17-18.

The same principle applies to renewing our minds; thinking about it reveals our desire to change, but without taking action, nothing will happen.

You cannot change the past, but you can change the future by the decisions you make today. In her book, *You Can Heal Yourself,* Louise Hay says, "Every thought you think is creating your future."

Thoughts can be habit-forming and direct our lives; they are not just fleeting ideas, but create patterns that will either limit or empower us. Our thoughts are influenced from an early age, so it's essential to consider our background to understand how we think and act, as well as what needs to change.

How has your background affected you?

We have all been influenced by our background. The way we were raised determines how we think, which in turn shapes our belief systems and causes us to act in specific ways. This is a result of both positive and negative inputs into our lives.

These experiences will range from soul-destroying thoughts spoken over your life —such as "You will never amount to anything" — to positive, affirming words like "You can change the world." These thoughts begin to shape your life from an early age.

Although you may be a product of the past, you do not have to be a prisoner of it. When you come to faith in Christ, you can break free from the past because the past is gone, and you are a new creation in Christ. This is your legal position, and nothing can change that - but in reality, you still have to renew your mind.

We have all been impacted in some way by our school years. They are usually a mixture of positive and negative experiences. We may have been praised or put down.

I remember my high school science teacher, who knew his lessons by heart. He would ask a student to read the last paragraph from the previous lesson before moving on to the next one. One day, he pointed to me and asked me to read the previous paragraph. I apologised and said, "I'm sorry, but I took my book home to do some homework and forgot to bring it." He scolded me in front of the class and said in a demeaning manner, "Boyle, what is the foreman going to say when you leave school and get a job filling in potholes on the road, and you say to him, "I'm sorry, I forgot my pick and shovel?" He was trying to embarrass me so that I would remember to bring my science book in future.

There was another time when we were told to stand in front of the class and give a two- to five-minute talk on our favourite subject. I spoke about fishing, but after a minute, I felt intimidated as I looked at the rest of the class. I had a brain freeze, stumbled over my words, became embarrassed, and sat down. I thought to myself, I will never speak in public again. But God had other ideas. Years later, when God called me to the ministry, I prayerfully replayed this incident in my mind. Being embarrassed, I sat back down at my school desk. Jesus walked into the room, looked around at all the students, then pointed at me and said, "I have chosen you to preach the gospel - Follow me."

When it comes to public speaking, American film director John Ford said, "You can speak well if your tongue can deliver the message of your heart." Something worth remembering if you desire to speak in public. Jesus said, *"For out of the abundance of the heart the mouth speaks."* Matthew 12:34.

Why do we remember embarrassing incidents? We feel ridiculed, devalued, and humiliated in front of others, which can lead to feelings of guilt and shame. Instead of dwelling on these negatives, we must learn to bounce back after our ego and self-confidence are knocked down — like children's building blocks — and pick ourselves up to rebuild and become positive again.

Our parents have a profound influence on our lives, whether direct or indirect. I was fortunate enough to have fairly positive parents. They were also affirming, something I now value. Even though I was not raised in a typical, dedicated Christian family, my parents were God fearing, and they always loved and affirmed me.

My mother was loving, and I spent a lot of time with my father; we did lots of things together. If he asked me to do something and I became negative, saying, "I can't do it," he would say, "There is no such word as can't, you will not find it in the dictionary." He was right because I tried to find it in several dictionaries at the time. However, it may be included in some today. Since becoming a Christian, I have learned to match any sayings I come across, such as the one my father mentioned —"There is no such word as can't" — with positive scriptures like *"I can do all things through Christ who strengthens me."* Philippians 4:13. So, instead of saying "I can't," I say, "I'm a can-do person."

We need to have not only belief and confidence in God but also in ourselves. We should say things like, "You can if you think you can." In his book *Awaken the Giant Within*, Tony Robbins says, "If you can't, you must. If you must, you can." He says the only limits to your impact in life are your imagination and commitment; you need both to succeed.

My late sister Lyn was five years older than I. When she was younger, she was a fastidious eater, especially with certain vegetables. Much to my parents' dismay, this had a profound effect on me, as I would mimic her by refusing to eat the same vegetables she did. It took me years to overcome some of those bad habits. These days, much to the delight of my wife and family, I will eat almost anything.

As a young person, I was greatly influenced by peer pressure from my friends, and to be accepted, I would often copy what they thought, said, and did.

When we become Christians, we recognise the need to

overcome past negative influences that have shaped our thinking and to focus on renewing our minds and belief systems, aligning our thoughts with Scripture.

Stop dwelling on the negatives

As a result of negative input into our lives, we may do things right and still not receive compliments or affirmations. However, instead of dwelling on them, we are inclined to focus on the one mistake or negative comment directed at us.

A lady approached me after I preached one time and said, "Your message was simple but good." Guess what I remembered? Yes, the word 'simple.'

What keeps us awake at night? It is usually the one negative thing that has happened rather than the many positive things we have accomplished. We mentally tend to beat ourselves up over minor things.

The greatest forms of stress we encounter are our interactions with other people. You cannot control what they say and do. But you can control the space they occupy in your mind and how much you let them stress you out.

Winston Churchill, in one of his speeches, quoted someone as saying, "You will never get to the end of the journey if you stop to throw stones at every dog that barks." In other words, do not be distracted by negative things said about you or your vision.

Sometimes when people turn to Christ, they have been in

bondage to all kinds of sinful activities. You may have been abused or abusive, and it has impacted your mind to the extent that you need healing or deliverance, either spiritually or by professional help. We cannot change the past, but we can change the present that will shape our future. When the devil intimidates us by reminding us of past mistakes, we need to say, *"Do not rejoice over me, my enemy; When I fall, I shall arise; When I sit in darkness, the Lord shall be a light unto me."* Micah 7:8.

The truth sets us free

Some people come from a background of lying to make themselves feel good. Christians have no reason to tell lies. I was recently looking through some old National Geographic magazines and came across the cover title "Why Do We Tell Lies?" It was a scientific investigation into the reason we tell lies. It was found that most of us start lying between the ages of 2 and 10. The article explained how we tell lies to get our own way. "As we age, we continue to do the same, but become more adept and skilled at the process. We tell lies to feel good about ourselves and to reach our goals. If the truth does not work in our favour, then we revert to lying to achieve our purpose." From a biblical perspective, Jesus told us that lies originate from the devil. Therefore, to understand the negative consequences of lying, we must return to the beginning, where we find the devil deceiving Eve in the Garden of Eden. The devil said to Eve, **"Has God indeed said**, *you shall not eat of every tree of the Garden?"* Genesis 3:1. When Eve replied, *"We are not to eat from the tree in the middle of the garden lest we die"*, the devil came back with another twist to sow more doubt. *"You shall not surely die."* (3:4). The devil was lying, by implying that God is good and he will not kill you, so go ahead and eat. They did, and as a result, sin, guilt, shame and death entered the world.

If we are to avoid guilt and shame as Christians today, we need to know the truth about **"What has God said about who we are in Christ?"** I will mention a few things that God says about us in Christ: we are 'redeemed and forgiven,' 'a new creation,' 'chosen and adopted as sons and daughters of God,' 'joint heirs with Christ,' 'free from condemnation,' 'loved by God,' 'blessed with every spiritual blessing,' 'more than conquerors,' 'seated in heavenly places,' 'sealed with the Holy Spirit,' and 'citizens of heaven.'

Jesus said, *"You shall know the truth and the truth will make you free."* John 8:32. I had a woman manifest during an altar call. In a weird voice, she said, "I can't stand your preaching." (not the sort of thing you want to hear) I said, "Why is that?" To which she replied, putting her hands over her ears, "Too much truth, I can't stand the truth." The devil hates the truth, so we should love it, embrace it, believe it, and confess it.

Once we have been set free, we have a responsibility to stand on the truth of God's word and stay free from past bondages. *"Stand fast therefore in the liberty by which Christ has made us free, and do not be entangled again with a yoke of bondage."* Galatians 5:1.

As a Christian, when we face temptation, or negative memories and thoughts, we have the right to go on the attack and rebuke and condemn whatever the enemy might throw at us, whether verbal, emotional, physical or spiritual. *"No weapon formed against you shall prosper, and every tongue which rises against you in judgment you shall condemn. This is the heritage of the servants of the Lord, and their righteousness is from Me."* Isaiah 54:17. So, every tongue that rises against you, that accuses you, and judges you, be it human or demonic, you have the right to condemn it. You do not have to put up with it because you are justified and made righteous by the righteousness of God through your faith in Christ.

Never give up, dwell on future possibilities

There are many stories of people who, despite past failures and negative experiences, such as rejection, refused to give up and instead focused on future possibilities. Before J.K. Rowling became one of the most successful authors in history, she faced a long series of personal and professional hardships. Rowling was a single mother surviving on government assistance. She was divorced, struggling with depression and trying to raise her daughter while working on a book idea that had come to her on a delayed train ride: the story of a young boy who discovered he was a wizard.

She wrote most of the Harry Potter books in cafés, often pushing a stroller beside her and scribbling notes when she could find time. When the manuscript was finally finished, she submitted it to multiple publishers and was rejected by twelve of them. They told her that children's books about wizards would never sell. Still, Rowling refused to give up. Finally, Bloomsbury, a small British publishing house, gave her a chance.

YOUR THOUGHTS SHAPE YOUR LIFE

The rest is history. The Harry Potter series sold more than 500 million copies and evolved into a successful film franchise.

Although I'm not a fan of the Harry Potter series, I use it as an example to show that when you're frustrated and think you're not making any headway, never give up.

Chapter 3

You may not be as perfect as you think

I had to laugh at a recent Facebook post in which a lady was crying because her husband told her he loved her despite all her imperfections. She was crying because she thought she had none.

We may not be as perfect as we think, because we all have blind spots that are obvious to God and others but not to ourselves. However, God, by His grace, still chooses to use us despite our imperfections.

My wife and I were ministering in a village in Vanuatu some years ago, and one of the leaders asked me how old I was. I said, "Have a guess?" He said, "Seventy." In shock, I said, "What about my wife?" He replied, "Seventy-five." We were both nudging fifty at the time. In that culture, older people are shown more respect and honour.

When someone points out our flaws, it doesn't mean we should disqualify ourselves; it is just a fact of life. American novelist *Edgar Howe* said, "We should express a mean opinion of ourselves occasionally, it will show our friends that we know how to tell the truth."

If only we could maintain a perfect image of ourselves. On a bright, calm, sunny day, we say, "What a perfect day." We probably wish every day were perfect, but if every day were perfect, there would be no bad days to compare them to.

What about our downcast days?

Some Christians are in denial by confessing that they never have any. They may be rare, but if we are honest, we all have them. Even the apostle Paul had them.

"When we came to Macedonia, our bodies had no rest, but we were troubled on every side. Outside were conflicts, inside were fears. Nevertheless, God, who comforts the downcast, comforted us by the coming of Titus." 2 Corinthians 7:6. Paul was downcast because they were physically and spiritually tired and worn out. The word downcast means to be depressed, disillusioned, and humiliated. This is the apostle Paul, who wrote such positive things as *"Rejoice in the Lord always and again I say rejoice."* How did God comfort him on this occasion? By the coming of Titus. Titus brought them good news about how the church had responded positively to Paul's first letter to the Corinthians, which instructed them to set things in order. This not only comforted Paul but also caused him to rejoice again. God can send us the right person at the right time with the right message to

turn our lives around when we are downcast. We should value the timely input of others who can bring us comfort.

Tough times help us appreciate the good times, failure helps us appreciate success, and sickness helps us appreciate health. Our imperfections help us appreciate the amazing grace of God that perfects us in Christ. The apostle Paul says, "Not that I have already attained, or am already perfected; but I press on, that I may lay hold of that for which Christ Jesus has also laid hold of me." Philippians 3:12.

Our past and present imperfections can leave an indelible impression on our minds, which we can overcome through Christ. This raises another challenging question I will address under the following heading.

Can the Holy Spirit dwell in imperfect vessels?

The reality is that we are not perfect compared to the Holiness of God. So, this means that at times the Holy Spirit must use imperfect vessels; otherwise, He would dwell in no one because no one is perfect or without sin.

These thoughts may shock some of you, but before you condemn me, let me clarify my statement. We need to realise that none of us are Holy by our merit; we have been forgiven and cleansed by the blood of Christ through the redemptive work of the cross. We have become a new creation in Christ. This is our spiritual status in Christ, and nothing can change that.

However, we still have a problem, it is called the flesh.

The apostle Paul wrestles with this problem when he says, *"For I know that in me (that is, in my flesh) nothing good dwells; for to will is present with me, but how to perform what is good I do not find." "For the good that I will to do, I do not do; but the evil I will not to do, that I practice."* Romans 7:18-19.

Paul is saying this in the context that the law cannot save us from sin; our only hope is to turn to Christ.

We are still fragile (fleshly) vessels of clay. *"We have this treasure in earthen vessels, that the excellence of the power may be of God and not of us."* 2 Corinthians 4:7. Our flesh is frail, and while in our earthly bodies, we continue to be subject to the temptations of the flesh.

Jesus said to His disciples, *"Watch and pray, lest you enter into temptation. The spirit indeed is willing, but the flesh is weak."* Matthew 26:41. Although we may be strong in spirit, the flesh is still weak.

What does it mean to walk in the Spirit?

The last thing Jesus instructed His disciples to do before He ascended back to heaven was to be filled with the Holy Spirit. This occurred on the day of Pentecost, when they were all gathered in Jerusalem and praying together. *"And they were all filled with the Holy Spirit and began to speak with other tongues, as the Spirit gave them utterance."* Acts 2:4. From that moment on, they became so dependent upon the power, gifts and guidance of the Holy Spirit. So, being filled with the Holy Spirit today will help us to walk in the Spirit.

Just because we are filled with the Holy Spirit does not guarantee that we will overcome fleshly desires; we still have to do our part by resisting temptation, but being filled with the Holy Spirit undoubtedly helps us live as overcomers.

"Walk in the Spirit, and you shall not fulfil the lusts of the flesh. For the flesh lusts against the Spirit and the Spirit against the flesh; and these are contrary to one another, so that you do not do the things that you wish." Galatians 5:16-17.

Walking in the Spirit involves avoiding sinful desires by obeying and applying the word of God. *"How can a young man cleanse his way? By taking heed according to Your word."* Psalm 119:9.

The Christian church is continually being washed clean as we walk in the Spirit and the Word simultaneously. This is an ongoing process until the return of Christ. *"Christ sanctifies and cleanses the church with the washing of water by the word that He might present it to Himself a glorious church, not having spot or wrinkle or any such thing, that she should be holy and without blemish."* Ephesians 5:26-27.

We all need the Holy Spirit to indwell us, enabling us to live a sanctified life by walking in the Spirit. We are not capable of doing this in our own strength because we are all, to some extent, marred or imperfect vessels. However, this is no excuse for living an unholy life, because God expects us to be Holy as He is; but that is only possible with the help of the Holy Spirit.

Are you waiting to be perfect?

If you are waiting to be perfect before God can use you, or to find the perfect church to join, you will be waiting a long time. The church is filled with imperfect people who say and do things they shouldn't. We can become hurt, wounded, offended and discouraged unless we face this reality and learn to overcome it. C. S. Lewis said, "God works on us in all sorts of ways...above all He works on us through each other." Sometimes we are the ones who need to change. Whatever you are struggling with, let me assure you, God loves you and still desires to use you.

Examples of God using imperfect vessels

David, who had a heart after God. He loved God, and God loved him, but he still committed adultery with Bethsheba. Then, David had her husband, Uriah, deliberately killed so he could marry his wife. When his sin of adultery and murder was exposed, he cried out to God for forgiveness and restoration.

"Create in me a clean heart, O God, and renew a steadfast spirit within me. Do not cast me away from your presence, and do not take your Holy Spirit from me." Psalm 51:10-11.

Did God withdraw His presence and take away His Holy Spirit from David because of this? No, despite David's sin, he humbled himself before God, was remorseful and repentant, and God showed him mercy and grace. But David paid the price for his sin with the death of his child, born to Bethsheba. However, God restored his role as King over Israel and subsequently His relationship with God Himself.

Peter, who witnessed the miraculous catch of fish when Jesus asked him to put down the nets for a catch, realised he was in the presence of the Messiah.

"When Simon Peter saw it, he fell on his knees, saying, 'Depart from me, for I am a sinful man, O Lord!" Luke 5:8. Peter thought that he was too sinful to be a disciple, but what did Jesus do? Did he say to Peter, "You sure got that right, you had better stick to your fishing?" No, He chose Peter to be one of his followers and said, "From now on, you will catch men."

Paul witnessed the death of Stephen (who some regard as the first Christian martyr). Paul was on a mission to persecute the Christians, but was himself converted to Christianity after God intervened in his life. But Paul was well aware of his past and later wrote -

"I am the least of the apostles, who am not worthy to be called an apostle, because I persecuted the church of God. But by the grace of God, I am what I am, and his grace toward me was not in vain." 1 Corinthians 15:9-10.

Did God disregard Paul and say, "You are not worthy to be an apostle?" Did God seek someone with a clean slate who had no problems with Christianity? No, God deliberately chose Paul despite his past record of persecuting Christians and the church.

In case you are thinking, does all this mean God turns a blind eye to sin? Think again. God hates sin, but makes a way for us not to be slaves to sin.

He gives us dominion over sin, for we are no longer under the law but under His grace and able to overcome sin.

Let your conscience be your guide

How do we know if you are walking in the Spirit? Your conscience will remind you. Paul repeatedly emphasises the importance of walking before God and men with a clear conscience. Paul indicates that the Holy Spirit helps him to do this: *"I tell the truth in Christ, I am not lying, my conscience also bearing me witness in the Holy Spirit."* Romans 9:1.

Paul is convinced that a clear conscience motivates him to live with integrity and faith — spiritually and ethically — before God and men, and that the Holy Spirit helps him do so. *"I myself always strive to have a conscience without offence toward God and men."* Acts 24:16. Paul writes to Timothy, his son in the faith, to remind him of the importance of maintaining a clear conscience.

"Having faith and a good conscience, which some have rejected concerning the faith, have suffered shipwreck." 1 Timothy 1:19. Some have suffered shipwreck (not literally); it simply means they have gone astray and wrecked their lives because they failed to maintain a clear conscience. How do we maintain a clear conscience? It is by being sensitive to the Holy Spirit, who reminds us of the truth that will convict us of sin if we are tempted to go astray (John 16:7-13).

Therefore, we need a sound understanding of the truth,

which entails examining our belief system and renewing our minds to cultivate positive thoughts that can shape our future. This gives us a sure foundation for our thoughts, emotions, actions and behaviour.

Throughout this book, we will focus on the process of changing our belief system in conjunction with the word of God and with the help of the Holy Spirit.

YOUR THOUGHTS SHAPE YOUR LIFE

Chapter 4

God can do more than you imagine

Your imagination can help you to succeed; it allows you to dream, invent, and express ideas in all fields of life. You can mentally rehearse different scenarios. When I stare at a blank canvas, I use my imagination to create an image in my mind, which I hope to then translate into a work of art.

The scientist Albert Einstein did what was known as "Thought Experiments." One of these he records as riding alongside a beam of light—a mental image that led to his theory of relativity. He often said, "Imagination is more important than knowledge." I do not pretend to understand his theory entirely, but profound truths can be discovered through both imagination and logic.

Before aeroplanes existed, Wilbur and Orville Wright used their imagination to dream of human flight. They studied birds, designed gliders, and devised methods for controlling an aircraft, ultimately building one of the first aircraft to successfully fly.

C.S. Lewis created the world of Narnia using his vivid imagination, featuring talking animals, to entertain both children and adults while conveying profound spiritual truths reminiscent of Christ and His kingdom.

Spiritually, imagination allows us to visualise unseen realities, including the many promises of God that relate to the gospel, such as eternal life and heaven.

Allow your imagination to run wild

When you put your faith in God, He can do more through you than you can imagine or think possible.

*"Now to Him who is able to do **exceedingly abundantly above all that we ask or think**, according to the power that works in us, to Him be glory in the church by Jesus Christ to all generations. Forever and ever. Amen."* Ephesians 3:20-21. "He can do exceedingly abundantly above all that we ask or think," in the Greek, it is *hyper ek perissou;* it is not just "more," but a hyper extension, or immeasurably more, referring to God's limitless power.

His ability exceeds our wildest expectations. Therefore, we should think that God can do way beyond our limitations. Where does the power come from? "According to the power that works in us," this refers to the Holy Spirit who indwells the believer. It is not just God's power out there somewhere for us to find, but His power that works "in us." The challenge for us is to exercise our faith and tap into this power.

When God called me to attend Bible College, preparing me to become a pastor, a missionary, and start a Bible College in a foreign country, and minister throughout that nation, and to pastor a great church, act as chairman of a Christian School board, serve as an executive member of a movement, mentor other pastors, and write books, I needed plenty of imagination because I knew my limitations. I could have thought, "No, I am not capable of doing any of those things," ignored the call of God and missed out on the adventures of a lifetime.

Do what He tells you to do

After fishing all night and catching nothing, Peter was very sceptical when Jesus told him to launch out into the deep and put down the nets for a catch.

"Launch out into the deep and let down your nets for a catch." But Simon answered and said to Him, "Master, we have toiled all night and caught nothing; nevertheless, at Your word I will let down the net." And when they had done this, they caught a great number of fish, and their net was breaking. So, they signalled to their partners in the other boat to come and help them. And they came and filled both boats, so they began to sink." Luke 5:4-6.

Initially, Peter was negative: "We have fished all night and caught nothing." Thinking it would be a waste of time, he was imagining an empty net. In contrast, Jesus had the faith to envision a net full of fish. Peter relented and agreed to do what Jesus had asked. When they pulled the nets in, they were overflowing with fish. So, God did far more than Peter could have imagined.

Perhaps God is prompting you to cast your net in a specific direction. If you are sceptical, like Peter, you may need to say something like, "Nevertheless, at your word, I will do what you tell me."

Think about sound investment strategies

There came a time when my wife and I felt compelled to cast our net into investing for the future. It is worth mentioning at this stage that when we inherited some money from our parents, we sought the Lord's guidance on what to do with it. We felt led to invest in blue-chip shares and property. This was a bold step, as we were in ministry and, in our circles at the time, there was an expectation that you were to live by faith on the smell of an oily rag and give your money away. However, by acting in faith and investing, we could never have imagined how beneficial that would become later in life as we faced retirement.

Jesus, in the parable of the talents (Matthew 25), instructs us to invest wisely. Talents can represent material and spiritual blessings. The instruction is to invest to make a profit. Jesus rebukes those who do nothing with their talent, burying or hiding it, and explains that the least they could have done was put it in the bank to earn interest. He calls them unprofitable servants. So, the implication is that you work for money, but then you should make your money work for you by investing it. The same principle applies to other talents or gifts you may possess. Jesus is admonishing his servants to be faithful and profitable servants in the kingdom of God.

A lack of imaginative faith can lead to unbelief

Sometimes we are inclined to think that unbelief means we don't believe at all. However, that is not the case; unbelief is wrong believing, and it can lead to diminished faith. Jesus encountered this problem while ministering in his hometown of Nazareth, where he had grown up. It seems that familiarity with Jesus and His family, seeing Him as one of them, created an atmosphere of unbelief.

"When Jesus came to Nazareth, where He grew up, He taught in the synagogue, and they were amazed and said, "Is this not the carpenter's son? Is not his mother called Mary? And His brothers, James, Joses, Simon, and Judas, and His sisters, are they not all with us? Where then did this man get all these things? So, they were offended at Him. But Jesus told them, "A prophet is not without honour except in his own country, and in his own house." Now, He did not do many mighty works there because of their unbelief." Matthew 13:54-58.

They thought he was just one of them, the carpenter's son. We know Mary, His mother, and his brothers and sisters. Some of them had trouble believing that He could be the Messiah. So, because of their unbelief and a lack of faith, He could not do many mighty works. We probably all need help overcoming our unbelief at times. The disciples had trouble casting out a demon from a boy. When the father took the boy to Jesus, the boy convulsed and fell on the ground and wallowed, foaming at the mouth. Jesus said to the father, "If you can believe all things are possible to him who believes." Immediately, the father of the child said with tears, "Lord, I believe, help my unbelief." Mark 9:20-25. Like some of us, the father was probably so focused on the problem he had lived with for years, rather than having the imagination and faith in Jesus to visualise the boy being set free and made whole. However, Jesus cast out the spirit and the boy was set free and healed.

Your faith produces results

"Faith…is the confident assurance that something we want is going to happen." Hebrews 11:1 (TLB). It is a strong conviction based on the word of God. It is such a firm conviction within us that persuades us to believe. It is not based on our intellect, emotions, or denomination. It is based on the Word of God that inspires us to keep thinking by faith until we see it happen. The timing is in God's hands.

In Hebrews 11, we read a list of names commonly called the "Heroes of faith," who accomplished great things by faith, thereby pleasing God. They were visionaries who could imagine and visualise the promises of God and the reward that awaited them if they obeyed Him by faith. It is impossible to believe in God without faith. *"Without faith it is impossible to please Him, for he who comes to God must believe that he is and that he is a rewarder of those who diligently seek Him."* Hebrews 11:6. I will list a few of these great heroes of faith and make some comments for you to ponder.

By faith, Enoch lived a life that pleased God amidst a wicked generation. He is an exception because he did not see death. God took him because God was pleased with his faith, compared to the evil generation in which he lived.

By faith, Noah, being divinely warned by God, built an

ark to save his family and the animals when the flood came. Noah built it according to the blueprint God gave him. People mocked him for doing it, but he acted in faith, likely because he had never seen a flood.

By faith, Abraham obeyed God when He asked him to leave his home and family to follow the Lord to an unknown destination.

By faith, Sarah received strength for childbearing after she had passed the age of childbearing. Although she sent Abraham to her servant to bear a child for them before the right time, God remained faithful to the promise, and she gave birth to a child of her own.

By faith, Moses forsook Egypt, where he had been raised. He obeyed God to lead the children of Israel out of slavery through instituting the Passover and opening the Red Sea to lead them to the promised land.

Not to mention a host of others listed, such as Joshua, Rahab, Gideon, Barak, Samson, Jephthah, David, Samuel, and the prophets. Many of these heroes of faith were not born that way. They were ordinary men and women like you and me. *"Out of weakness were made strong, became valiant in battle."* Hebrews 11:34. Because God was with them, they found that although they were weak, they became strong in battle. God ignited their faith and supernaturally empowered them. When you feel weak and unable to overcome in your own strength, call upon the mighty power of God to enable you to rise in faith and win the battle.

What can God do through you?

You may be thinking I do not have faith. Yes, you do! *"God has dealt to each one a measure of faith."* Romans 12:3. Faith was not reserved for those heroes we read about in the Bible. You have been given a measure of faith that you can stir up and put into practice.

You will be amazed at what God can do through you. If you make yourself available and let God stretch your imagination and faith, you'll find God can do far more than you could possibly think.

Chapter 5

The way you think affects your attitude

Your thoughts will affect your attitude regarding how you respond emotionally or behaviourally to situations.

Negative thinking leads to negative attitudes, feelings and behaviours such as frustration, anger, fear and anxiety. Positive, faith-filled thinking leads to peace, joy, and the confidence to make wise decisions.

I was watching "Britain's Got Talent," and a young contestant was very negative about herself. Simon Cowell responded, "You are not doing a very good job of selling yourself," suggesting she change her attitude. I immediately thought of a book I read some years ago called *How to Sell Yourself* by Joe Girard, reputed to be the world's best car salesman —a title given to him by the Guinness Book of World Records. I gained some insight from reading the first three chapters. The *first* chapter of the book was "Selling

Yourself on You," which is all about selling yourself. The *second* Chapter was "Selling yourself to others," which posed the question "Would anybody want to buy you?" (How to present yourself to others). The *third* chapter was about "Building self-confidence and courage." It explained how self-confidence breeds courage. Although it was a great read, endorsed by Norman Vincent Peale, who emphasises the importance of attitudes, I felt that much of the book relied more on self-effort than on the transforming power of God.

God inspired attitudes

When you face a problem, the problem itself is not always the problem; it is the attitude you have toward it. Your thoughts determine how you interpret and respond to a situation. You can transform your attitude into a more positive, helpful one by believing that all things are possible with God. By faith, consider all possible solutions to the problem.

In our endeavour to be positive, it is not just pretending everything is okay. We need to maintain our integrity by being honest and open about our struggles, suffering, pain, and not denying reality. To maintain a positive outlook, we sometimes think we need to be dishonest.

Positive thinking, from a Christian perspective, means having a clear conscience with both ourselves and others; our integrity is essential.

As we have already explained, the context of "As a man thinks in his heart, so is he" refers to a person with a hidden agenda. Although he appears accommodating outwardly, his heart is not with you. It is about potential betrayal and hypocrisy. We do not want to go down that path by outwardly putting on a positive front when all is not well, nor do we want to dwell on the negative. We need a healthy balance to our positive thinking, by exercising wise thoughts that maintain our integrity and authenticity through our connection with God, His Word, and His people.

Some years ago, I was ministering in Hyderabad, India. There was a Hindu Guru on television in the place where I was staying, and he was talking about the secret to happiness. He kept saying that to be happy, you must keep smiling and look happy regardless of your circumstances. However, his message was utterly detached from both reality and God. He was trying to convince people that by putting on a false front and continually smiling, he could convince himself and others that he was happy. *Russ Harris*, author of The Happiness Trap, writes, "So many people now think, "If I'm not happy, there is something wrong with me." "We seem to have forgotten that feelings are like the weather changing all the time; it's as normal to feel unhappy as it is to have rainy days."

Having said all that, is it possible to think yourself happy? The apostle Paul thought so despite being a prisoner in chains. However, you will see that the basis of his happiness is his faith in God, regardless of his circumstances. Let us examine the following scripture.

Can you think yourself happy?

The apostle Paul stood in chains before King Agrippa and

said, **"I think myself happy."** Was he being honest? What he said makes no sense. Why would he, as a prisoner in chains, be happy?

"Then Agrippa said to Paul, "You are permitted to speak for yourself." So, Paul stretched out his hand and answered for himself: **I think myself happy,** *King Agrippa, because today I shall answer for myself before you concerning all things of which I am accused by the Jews, especially because you are expert in all customs and questions which have to do with the Jews. Therefore, I beg you to hear me patiently."* Acts 26:1-3.

"I think myself happy" can be translated in Greek as "I consider myself fortunate," or I am glad." There is no denying his ability to think positively despite his situation. He had little to be happy about because he had been arrested and held in custody for the past two years in Caesarea, a Roman provincial capital. Paul could have seized the opportunity to ask to be released or complain about his imprisonment and the treatment he received. But he is more than happy to have the chance to speak publicly and share the gospel directly with the King.

His positive attitude is not detached from God or reality; he is not putting on a false front; he is genuinely happy. He chooses not to dwell on his present state because he is overjoyed to be able to address the king and those in high places. He is fulfilling his calling and mission by preaching the gospel. Paul gives a lengthy discourse before the king, sharing his testimony, calling, and mission to present the gospel to both Jews and Gentiles. Therefore, the primary reason for

Paul's happiness is his personal relationship with Christ.

The king must have been impressed by Paul's discourse. As Paul finished his message, we read in verse 28, *"Then Agrippa said to Paul, "You almost persuade me to become a Christian."* You almost persuaded me! How close he came to becoming a Christian! How many people today come so close to becoming a Christian and then decline? A decision they will regret when they enter eternity.

Paul responds to the king, saying, *"I would to God that not only you but also all who hear me today, might become almost and together such as I am, except for these chains."* Verse 29.

Paul is thankful for the opportunity to share the gospel, hoping that all of them will become Christians, except for the chains that bind him. When the leaders met later, they decided that Paul could have been set free if he had not chosen to appeal to Caesar (Verse 32). So, they had no option but to keep him in prison so he could eventually be sent to Rome.

When God called us to go to Papua New Guinea to start a Bible College, my wife and I had three children, and our fourth (Sharon) was born in PNG. We initially found it hard to adjust, being uprooted from Australia and leaving our parents and relatives behind to come to a potentially fearful, hostile environment. In his book *As a Man Thinketh*, James Allen says, "The soul attracts that which it secretly harbours; that which it loves, and also that which it fears."

At the time, to make things worse, the college building,

which was meant to be completed on our arrival, was only half-built, and a house to be built for us had not even begun. We commenced lectures at a scout camp just outside Port Moresby, in a mountainous, mosquito-infested jungle.

As a family, we lived in "leave houses" —houses people did not want to leave empty when they went away, due to the high crime rate. We moved almost every month for 12 months until our home was finished.

It would have been easy to spit the dummy, complain, and return to Australia because things weren't what we'd expected. However, we maintained a positive attitude because we believed we were in God's will.

Despite our circumstances, we considered ourselves happy to live in a foreign country, and as a result, the Bible College was a great success. Students were trained for ministry. God was pouring out His Spirit throughout the nation. People were turning to Christ, and many were healed and delivered from demonic oppression. They were exciting days. We were only meant to stay for one year, but we ended up staying for six years. Looking back, we are thankful we maintained a positive attitude and our integrity during this time.

Some attitudes need to change

We could examine many attitudes that need to change. One recent issue is the so-called "Sovereign Citizens." They are independent of government authority and subject only to their interpretation of the laws of the land, declaring themselves sovereign. They even claim their rights are God-given, not government-granted. However, only God is sovereign, and He has instituted government authorities for our safety. (Romans 13:1-7).

When we turn to faith in Christ, many worldly attitudes we have developed need to change. Peter writes to new Christians, challenging them to change certain attitudes by telling them to *"lay aside all malice, all deceit, hypocrisy, envy, and all evil speaking, as newborn babes desire the pure milk of the word, that you may grow thereby."* 1 Peter 2:1. These things are aspects of our unsanctified human nature. Let me elaborate on these for ease of understanding.

Malice – Wanting the worst for others.

Deceit – Failing to be truthful.

Hypocrisy – Failing to live by our own values.

Envy – A deeply felt desire to possess what others have.

Slander – Trashing others' reputations.

Nothing has changed; we still struggle with these attitudes in our society today. When we become Christians, Peter says we need to lay aside these attitudes and desire the pure milk of the word. He infers that continuing with these attitudes is immature, and we need to adhere to the fundamentals of the word to help us change and grow in faith.

How to strengthen your attitude

The bible declares, *"The joy of the Lord is your strength."* Nehemiah 8:10. Does this joy give us the strength to endure hardships? It is the joy of the Lord that makes the difference, not happiness based on circumstances. It is this joy that helps us to maintain a positive attitude.

Kay Warren, in her book *Choose Joy: Because Happiness isn't Enough*, says, "That while happiness is often contingent on external circumstances, true joy is a deeper, more resilient state rooted in one's faith and perspective."

She shares her journey, including the profound grief of losing her son to suicide, emphasising that choosing joy does not negate pain but offers a pathway through it, not denying hardships but embracing a perspective that sees beyond them. We need to realise that joy is not based on blind optimism that denies reality, but on faith-filled thinking that maintains a positive attitude.

The Bible tells us how to maintain a positive, joyful attitude, as outlined in Philippians 4:4-13. *"Rejoice in the Lord always. Again, I will say rejoice!"*

In this verse, we have a double emphasis on rejoicing in the Lord at all times. How can we do that when it seems we have nothing to rejoice about? We should follow these two steps -

Firstly, empty yourself of anxiety and worry –

Let go of anxiety and worry by emptying out those negative thoughts and concerns in prayer before God. We are told not to hold back but to pour out everything to God in prayer. *"Be anxious for nothing, but in everything by prayer and supplication, with thanksgiving, let your requests be made known to God; and the peace of God which passes understanding, will guard your hearts and minds through Christ Jesus."* Verses 6-7.

Continue to empty your mind of negative thoughts causing anxiety until the peace of God fills your heart and mind. Jesus told us not to worry about the basics we need in life, but to seek first the kingdom of God and His righteousness, and all these things shall be added to us. (Matthew 6:25-34).

Secondly, fill your mind by thinking about good things –

Replace those negative, discouraging, and demeaning thoughts that cause anxiety and worry with wholesome thoughts that are good and positive. Verse 8 says, *"Whatsoever things are true, whatsoever things are noble, whatsoever things are just, whatsoever things are pure, whatsoever things are lovely, whatsoever things are of good report, if there is any virtue and if there is anything praiseworthy - meditate on these things."*

To meditate or think on these things is to dwell on them and go over them in your mind, just like a cow chewing the cud, getting the sustenance and flavour you need for positive thinking.

The way you think can help change your attitude.

YOUR THOUGHTS SHAPE YOUR LIFE

Chapter 6

Your mind is not renewed overnight

If only we could renew our minds overnight. We live in an instantaneous society, and we hate waiting. We say things like, "Why is the microwave taking so long?" We have become so impatient that the only thing we do not seem to mind waiting for is a good cup of coffee.

We often think that renewing the mind is an instant, overnight, quick fix. Unfortunately, it is a process we must continually work on.

A 2020 study by psychologists at Queen's University in Canada employed a novel method to estimate thoughts based on brain pattern shifts, revealing that the average person has approximately 6,200 distinct thoughts per day. (This was previously thought to be around 60,000 to 70,000 per day).

Studies suggest that approximately 80% of our thoughts

are repetitive, and that around 60-70% of these are negative. This is referred to as the mind's "negativity bias." This is why it becomes essential to adopt a "positivity bias."

The scripture agrees with this because, as Christians, we are encouraged to renew our minds and free them from the world's negative influences.

"Do not be conformed to this world, but be transformed by the renewing of your mind, that you may prove what is that good and acceptable and perfect will of God." Romans 12:1-2.

Are you conforming or transforming?

Did you notice the two keywords in this process? Do not be conformed to this world, but be transformed by the renewing of your mind. So, let us consider this process.

Do not be conformed to this world –

Although we live in the world, we are not to conform to it, allowing it to continue shaping our thoughts, actions, behaviour, and identity through its culture, ungodly, sinful morals, and values. It is a system often separated from God because of pride, selfishness, and a materialistic outlook on life. However, this poses a question: "What is our image of God in this world today?" Some people tend to create their idea of God based on how they think He should be. They believe God should endorse the ways they consider acceptable for humanity to live. It is imagining God will even tolerate our immoral ways, so that no one is excluded from His love. This is called theistic humanism. These are people who believe they can discern what is best for themselves through human intellect and knowledge, rather than what God says in His Word. This is different to secular humanism that leaves God out of the picture altogether.

However, it is God who knows what is best for us, as revealed in the bible. The gospel (good news) is that Christ died for the whole human race on His terms, not ours. The grace of God is extended to all; it is our choice to respond in faith. We either conform to the humanistic ways of the world or embrace the ways of God. This means we need to renew our minds by understanding His ways so we can be transformed into His image.

Renewing our minds can be a slow process, I've heard described as dipping a spoon into a jar of honey, pulling it out, and watching it slowly drain away. Our worldly ways of thinking seem to depart slowly, just like the honey. We should not become frustrated; changing our belief system is a tedious process that feels like it is taking longer than anticipated. For us as Christians, this is all a part of renewing our minds.

Be transformed –

The Greek word for "transformed" is *metamorphoo*, the root of our word "metamorphosis." It implies a fundamental transformation, akin to a caterpillar gradually becoming a butterfly. Once again, we can see this is a process.

For us as Christians, it is an internal spiritual transformation that begins in the heart and mind. We could call this the "Butterfly Effect": how little changes can make a big difference, how an insignificant grub can become a beautiful butterfly.

The process varies for different individuals. When we are born again, our spirit comes alive, and we become a new person in Christ. Our mind seems to play a catch-up game with our spirit.

One thing I noticed changed instantly for me was that the moment I was born again, I stopped swearing. However, over the years, I have noticed that the odd, unsavoury word, which I find embarrassing, seems to slip out if I were to hit my finger with a hammer. This is an ongoing process that we must continue to refine and improve.

By the renewing of your mind –

Your thoughts are renewed as you transform your belief system into one that is continually replaced with new thought patterns grounded in the word of God. How does this work in reality? Let me give you a brief example.

If you're struggling with old thoughts from past experiences that still bother you, consider addressing them. They may have originated from a fear of rejection, disappointment, betrayal, grief, trauma, failure or pressure to measure up, but they leave you with feelings of guilt and shame, thoughts like -

> "You have made a mess of your life."
> "You will never be forgiven."
> "You will always fail."
> "You are not worthy to be loved."
> "You have no future."

Recognise these thoughts as intrusions into your life, and drive them out of your mind to align your thinking with God's word. Replace the thought (lie) with the word of God (truth). It sounds simple, but it requires discipline to do it.

Deliberately repeat what God says about you, like –
"There is no condemnation for those in Christ."
"I can do all things through Christ who strengthens me."
"Nothing can separate me from the love of God."
"God has not given me a spirit of fear."
"All things are possible with God."

Ask the Holy Spirit for help -

Jesus sent the Holy Spirit as our helper. Ask the Holy Spirit for guidance, and He will bring to your remembrance the appropriate scripture to affirm and repeat to yourself. One significant benefit of a renewed mind is that it enables us to discover God's will for our lives. As we continue reading Romans 12:2 and the following verses, the context reveals that a transformed mind leads to finding and understanding God's will and the potential ministry for our lives.

"Be transformed by the renewing of your mind, that you may prove what is that good and acceptable and perfect will of God." Romans 12:2.

What is the will of God for your life?

A renewed mind helps you think clearly, so you can discern what His will is for your life. How is that possible?

It is possible if we continue to study the following verses and come to an understanding of how they might apply to us. We may discover what a good fit for us is by how we can best serve the Lord.

"For I say through the grace given to me, to everyone who is among you, not to think of himself more highly than he ought to think, to think soberly, as God has dealt to each one a measure of faith. For we have many members in one body, but all the members do not have the same function." Verse 3-4.

So, the implication is that we should stay within the bounds of our measure of faith. This, in turn, will depend on the appropriate gift that suits us and with which we can feel comfortable functioning.

"Having then gifts differing according to the grace that is given to us." Verse 6. *It then lists seven gifts of grace: prophecy, ministry, teaching, exhortation, giving, leadership, and mercy."*

One or more of these gifts will be a fit for you to function in. These are different to the nine gifts of the Holy Spirit, but they should also be taken into consideration in discovering where you function best. By studying these, you will be able to find God's will and learn how to serve both God and people effectively. This is a lengthy and detailed study, which I describe in my books, *"Unlocking Your Purpose"* and *"But for the Grace of God Go I."*

Recalling positive things to mind

If we are to renew our minds successfully, we should be recalling positive things. Despite suffering, Jeremiah says in

Lamentations 3:21, *"This I recall to mind. Therefore, I have hope."* What does he recall to mind?

He reminds himself that he is not consumed because of God's mercy, compassion and faithfulness.

"Through the Lord's mercies, we are not consumed, Because His compassions fail not. They are new every morning; great is Your faithfulness. The Lord is my portion, says my soul, therefore I hope in Him." Lamentations 3:22-24.

What a great confession to start with every morning! The mercies and compassions of the Lord are new every morning. His soul says so; he verbally declares it to be so every morning. We need to do the same; you can start every day with a clean slate. Therefore, he places his hope in God. We also need to think this way. David has a similar attitude to Jeremiah; he begins speaking to his soul when he feels down.

"Why are you cast down, O my soul? And why are you disquieted within me? Hope in God, for I will yet praise him for the help of His countenance." Psalm 42:5.

By a deliberate act of faith, David changed his mood of depression, declaring his hope in God by being determined to praise Him regardless of his situation. You, too, have every reason to praise Him. Remember, God is for you, not against you, irrespective of your circumstances.

Remember, renewing your mind is a process. By faith, declare your hope in God, even in the face of negativity, and believe in a future filled with positive outcomes.

YOUR THOUGHTS SHAPE YOUR LIFE

Chapter 7

You can overcome negative thoughts

Overcoming negative thoughts does not mean we will never have them. After working on renewing our minds, it is surprising how some negative thoughts persist and keep popping up even when we think we are in control. When we try to take control of those thoughts, the harder we try, the harder it seems to become. They appear to be uncontrollable. Most people seem to think it is a matter of human nature and that we must accept it. However, we do not have to put up with them; we can overcome these negative thoughts. There is an answer to this dilemma. I came across an interesting double-page article in the Weekend section of the Gold Coast Bulletin on Saturday, June 14 2025, titled *"How to overcome negative thoughts."* Because I was writing this book, it caught my attention. It was a review of the book *Deep Resilience*, by Melli O'Brien, an internationally renowned mental health educator and coach. I will quote extracts from the newspaper article.

"Have you ever tried to stop thinking negatively, only to find the more you try to push them away, the stronger they become?" "This phenomenon is known as the White Bear effect, first demonstrated by researcher Daniel Wegner. Instead of trying to eliminate them, the key is to change your relationship to them."

The article then described three techniques to help you successfully strengthen your mental capacity.

1. *Unhook from your unhelpful thoughts* – Often, we assume that our thoughts are facts, but in reality, they are just mental events. When we become hooked on a negative thought, "I'm not good enough", we need to apply a technique called de-fusion, which is to defuse it by saying to ourselves: "It's just a thought, words in my mind." Then let it float away like a leaf down a stream.

2. *Redirection: Shift your mental focus using questions* – When we get caught in negative thinking, our mind tends to loop through the same thoughts, reinforcing stress, anxiety and self-doubt. To break the cycle, we need to redirect our attention with empowering questions. Instead of trying to stop the thought, ask questions: "What can I do to change the situation?" "What would I tell someone else to do?" "How can I learn from this?" "What am I grateful for?" Therefore, interrupt the negative thoughts and make room for a more balanced approach.

3. *Self-Compassion: Change how you talk to yourself* – Research

shows that self-criticism increases stress, while self-compassion helps build resilience and emotional balance. Are your thoughts filled with harsh self-judgment and criticism? "You're not good enough." Shift to a kinder perspective by using a self-compassion statement, "This is hard right now, but I'm doing my best, I am good enough, I can make it."

What about from a biblical perspective?

How does the Bible describe this process? It is very similar, although much more aggressive, as it employs spiritual warfare terminology to overcome and control persistent negative thoughts, which are referred to as "strongholds" — meaning they take a strong hold on the mind. These negative thoughts need to be replaced with positive thoughts from the Word of God. The harmful, random, repetitive, and potentially destructive thoughts (strongholds) need to be identified as our enemies and pulled down. We face a battle to take control of these thoughts. It is a process that we can master with the help of the Holy Spirit and through the application of God's Word.

After reading the following scripture, I will share with you a dramatic experience I had through a dream that made these verses very real to me.

"For though we walk in the flesh, we do not war after the flesh. For the weapons of our warfare are not carnal but mighty in God for pulling down strongholds; casting down arguments, and every high thing that exalts itself against the knowledge of God, bringing every thought into

captivity to the obedience of Christ." 2 Corinthians 10:3-5."

The reality of the weapons of our warfare for pulling down strongholds became real to me after I had been put in charge of a spiritual warfare prayer meeting where we would pray over the nation of Australia and stand against the powers of darkness. I was struggling with this concept until I had a dream. In my dream, I was the Prime Minister of Australia's personal bodyguard. I was living in a unit attached to his house. I looked out the window and saw a fleet of black objects resembling stealth bombers in formation. I knew immediately that they were spiritual forces of darkness. As I looked, two of these objects spotted me, peeled off and came straight for me. I took out my revolver and began shooting at them, but it made no difference. They came in through the window and began to crush my chest, and tried to strangle me. I thought that if I could only say the name of Jesus, I would be okay. By this time, my wife woke up and thought I was having a heart attack. I finally managed to say, "Jesus," and the attack stopped immediately. The objects fled in fear. The reality sank in: we are in a spiritual battle, and we are to use spiritual weapons. Carnal weapons have no part in this battle.

This raises the question, "Can demonic forces influence our thoughts and minds?" I believe they can, and we see this was the case when Jesus told the disciples he would be killed in Jerusalem. When Peter heard Him say that, he took Jesus aside and rebuked Him, saying to Him, "This is not going to happen to you" Jesus turned and said to Peter, *"Get behind me, Satan! You are an offence to me, for you are not mindful of the things of*

God, but the things of men." Matthew 16:23.

What about lustful thoughts?

Are lustful thoughts demonic? Jesus, in His Sermon on the Mount, addresses several areas in which the law is compared with His teachings. *"You have heard it was said to those of old, "You shall not commit adultery." But I say to you, "Whoever looks at a woman to lust for her has already committed adultery with her in His heart."* Matthew 5:27-28. Jesus is more focused on the real problem, the condition of the heart.

While pastoring, you would be surprised how many men came to me confessing they had a problem with lustful thoughts and desperately needed help, some thinking they had a demon. In some instances, there were demonic influences that required ministry. But Jesus is emphasising that sexual temptation is a human weakness outside of the sanctity of marriage and that adultery is unacceptable.

However, it is doubtful that we will put a complete stop to lustful thoughts because they seem to arise spontaneously and unbidden. They are an intrusion on our lives and need to be resisted. It is what we do with them that matters. We should stop entertaining such thoughts, dwelling on them, and being ruled by them; at all costs, we must avoid acting on them.

We need to immediately shift our focus to something else and replace lustful thoughts with prayerful ones, grounded in the word. *"Your word I have hidden in my heart, that I might not sin against you."* Psalm 119:11.

What are our spiritual weapons?

We have many spiritual weapons to equip us to stand against the enemy's opposition. We are to dress for battle as described in Ephesians 6:10-18, and use the appropriate spiritual weapons as we engage in warfare.

I will list some of these weapons below that we need to use as directed by the Holy Spirit in specific situations.

* The name of Jesus, the name above all names.
* The blood of Jesus for the forgiveness of sins.
* The Word of God, which is the sword of the Spirit.
* The shield of faith to quell the fiery darts of the enemy.
* The helmet of salvation that protects our minds
* And always praying in the Spirit.

We do not rely on worldly weapons and strategies, but instead on spiritual weapons and techniques that are strong enough to bind and demolish strongholds in our minds by casting down opposing arguments, destroying the devil's lies, and replacing them with the Word of God. Therefore, our thoughts become submissive to the authority of God's word.

Some practical steps that will help you

It may help you to try and identify these thoughts by thinking about analysing them as follows -

Categorise your thoughts –

- Are they tormenting thoughts from the past?

- Are they tormenting thoughts about the present?
- Are they tormenting thoughts about the future?
- Are they just ordinary, random thoughts?
- I use the word tormenting because that is what the enemy likes to do to you. "But the spirit of the Lord departed from Saul, and a distressing (tormenting) spirit troubled him." 1 Samuel 16:14.

Identify the thoughts that accuse and condemn you –

- There is a difference between condemnation and conviction. Conviction makes you feel sad and sorry for offending God and gives you the opportunity to repent. Condemnation makes you feel bad about who you are and leaves you feeling despair. You doubt that God loves you, forgives you, and you wrestle with sinful thoughts of lust, envy, and pride, which make you feel depressed and defeated. They are lies that oppose and resist the word of God. They make us feel unworthy of receiving God's help. I use the words 'accuse' and 'condemn' because that is what the enemy does. *"For the accuser (devil) of our brethren, who accused them before our God, day and night, has been cast down."* Revelation 12:10.

Aggressively take those rogue thoughts Captive –

- To stop those thoughts influencing you, take them captive at the point of the sword of the Spirit, the word of God (not at the point of a gun). Tell them that you have destroyed their strongholds and they are now prisoners of Jesus Christ, that Jesus is the truth and the truth has set you free, and they are forbidden to torment or condemn you.

Replace those tormenting thoughts with God's Word –

- With thoughts of grace and peace, as the Holy Spirit brings appropriate scriptures to mind. Meditation and verbal repetition can be beneficial. Repeat them as many times as needed for peace of mind. You must focus on Christ and His Word. A Practical example of replacement – When you have thoughts that doubt that God loves you, forgives you or accepts you. Stop and say that is not true because by faith I believe what God says, "He made us (me) accepted in the beloved. In Him we (I) have redemption through His blood, the forgiveness of sins, according to the riches of His grace." Ephesians 1:6-7.

Several kings mentioned in the Old Testament did what was right in the eyes of the Lord. In each case, they played a crucial role in removing the altars dedicated to foreign gods. When our youngest grandson was named Asa, I was surprised to discover that the name originated from the Bible. Asa was one of these kings who did right in the eyes of the Lord. *"Asa removed the altars to the foreign gods and the high places and broke down the sacred pillars and cut down the wooden images. He commanded Judah to seek the Lord God of their fathers and to observe the law and the commandment."* 2 Chronicles 14:2-4.

I see a spiritual similarity in us doing what is right in the sight of the Lord by pulling down the strongholds in our minds (foreign gods or demonic influences), and then seeking to replace them with the Word of God.

Yes, it is possible to take control of our negative thoughts and replace them with positive ones that strengthen our faith in God.

YOUR THOUGHTS SHAPE YOUR LIFE

Chapter 8

A good report can impact many lives

A good report can impact many lives, including your own, as well as individuals, companies, organisations, and churches. It can boost self-esteem, increase energy levels, and project a more positive outlook for the future. We need to understand that positive words have tremendous power to attract people, whereas negativity tends to repel people and have no impact.

    I received a negative medical report some years ago when I was diagnosed with prostate cancer. This affected my faith because I had been praying and expecting a positive report. I was in shock when my PSA level kept rising to dangerous levels. So, I opted to follow medical advice and have the prostate removed. The result was mixed; they managed to preserve my nerves in that area, but the PSA, although initially considerably lower, continued to rise. After prayer and seeking God for wisdom, I decided to take the specialist's advice and have radiation treatment with some hormone injections. It was not a pleasant experience, but after the treatment, the result was excellent: my PSA level dropped to zero, and the nerves remained intact. This positive (excellent) report had the power to change my outlook on life; it had a profound impact on my faith, my family, and friends who had been praying for me.

A good report has a ripple effect on many people. There is an interesting example of this after Jesus healed a deaf mute: *"He commanded them that they should tell no one; but the more He commanded them, the more widely they proclaimed it."* Mark 7:36.

Even though they were told not to tell anyone, it is almost impossible to keep good news quiet. The news was so powerful that it spread like wildfire. Why did Jesus tell them not to tell anyone? Was he using reverse psychology, knowing the news would spread rapidly so more would come and be healed, or did he want to protect the identity of the deaf mute and his family? Or did he not want to draw too much attention to himself, knowing it would stir up those in authority who could have killed him before His time? We need to ask ourselves what God expect a good report to look like. A negative report to God contradicts the word of God; it can create fear and be destructive. In contrast, a positive report can be life-changing in all aspects of life, whether in leadership, business, personal development, or our spiritual walk as Christians.

How does God view a good or a bad report?

It is by what we say and how we say it. People are influenced by what they hear, especially from reliable, trusted sources. To illustrate my point, we have the classic story of the twelve spies whom God sent to spy out the Promised Land.

God sent one leader from each of the twelve tribes of Israel to spy out the Promised Land of Canaan, which they intended to invade and possess. Their mission was to scout the land, assess the strength of the people, determine if their cities were fortified, and evaluate the quality of the land, bringing back some of its fruit. After forty days, the spies returned and confirmed that the land flowed with milk and honey, bringing back clusters of grapes to prove it. However, ten spies spread fear, saying the people are powerful, that some giants inhabit the land, and we felt like grasshoppers in their sight; they live in fortified, walled cities. They said we cannot go up against the people, for they are stronger. All this was true, but God called it a bad report (or, in some translations, an evil report). What they were saying to the people was creating fear because it contradicted what God had told them to do: go in and possess the land.

However, two of the spies, Caleb and Joshua, gave a good report. *"Caleb quieted the people before Moses, and said, "Let us go up at once and take possession, for we are well able to overcome it."* Numbers 13:30.

What Caleb said, God called a good report because it indicated that they could fulfil what God had promised to do through them. Caleb was encouraging them to get on with it!

However, as a result, the children of Israel would not enter the Promised Land except for Joshua and Caleb, who gave a favourable report and stood against the negative report of the other ten spies. These spies had influenced the people to rebel against Moses and prompted them to seek another leader. But God did not allow it to happen. He was pleased with Caleb, saying he had a different spirit from the others.

"But my servant Caleb, because he has a different spirit in him and has followed Me fully, I will bring into the land where he went, and his descendants shall inherit it." Numbers 14:24. What does it mean to have a different spirit? It refers to our heart attitude toward God. It is someone dedicated, faithful and courageous compared to others who are unfaithful, fearful and rebellious.

From my experience working with other leaders and elders in the ministry, I know how influential a positive report can be in encouraging the church. It can filter through the church and affect the whole congregation. On the other hand, a negative report can have the opposite effect, discouraging the congregation.

A positive report can be a game-changer. Martin Luther changed the course of history for Christianity when he nailed his theses to the door of the Catholic Church in 1517, challenging the practice of indulgences and declaring that the "just shall live by faith." This marked the beginning of the Reformation, which challenged long-standing traditions and led to significant changes.

The power of your tongue - What you say is vital!

The Bible says that your words have the power to give life or take it away. *"Death and life are in the power of the tongue, and those who love it will eat its fruit."* Proverbs 18:21. Your words can bring death through your negative speech, characterised by lies, deceit, gossip, slander, rebellion, and pride, or they can bring life through your love, encouragement, truth, and wisdom. What are you speaking into your future? Your family? Your Career? Your finances? Your health? Instead of complaining and saying things like "I'm a born loser." "Things never seem to work out for me." Be positive and say things like "God is in control, when one door closes another will open." God will use it for my good."

What we say is vital if we are to live victoriously. *"Let the weak say I am strong."* Joel 3:10. It does not say let them dwell on their weakness and talk about it. Let them say the opposite of what they feel. Dwell on the fact that you are strong in the Lord. Talk about what strengths you have instead of your weaknesses. Start your day by saying, *"This is the day the Lord has made, I will rejoice and be glad in it."* Psalm 118:24. This will help change your attitude. When Jesus talks about faith, He says, *"….he will have whatever he says."* Mark 11:23.

If someone said something negative to us as children, we would shrug it off by saying, "Sticks and stones may break my bones, but words will never hurt me." We were putting on a bold front because negative words do hurt us, just as positive words can encourage us. We are responsible for what we say and should speak wisely, taking control of our tongue.

The book of James has more to say on this matter.

"The tongue is a little member and boasts great things. See how great a forest a little fire kindles!" James 3:5.

As a boy, I recall being in the car with my father on a sweltering day. We were returning from a fishing trip near the Grampian Mountains in Victoria when my father suddenly slammed on the brakes, having spotted a grass fire in the paddock. He jumped out of the car, telling me to stay there. He grabbed an empty wheat bag out of the boot, jumped over the fence, and ran into the paddock to try to extinguish the rapidly spreading grass fire. Other cars stopped, and several people joined him. However, the fire had escaped into the foothills and had become uncontrollable. We later discovered that a spark from a nearby tractor had ignited the fire. Unfortunately, a large number of sheep, cattle, and wildlife were lost.

The tongue can be like a wild bushfire out of control, causing significant damage. We are told that no one can tame the tongue, because it is unruly and unpredictable; it can bless God and curse people at the same time.

"No man can tame the tongue. It is an unruly evil, full of deadly poison. With it we bless our God and Father, and with it we curse men, who have been made in the similitude of God. Out of the same mouth proceed blessing and cursing. My brethren, these things ought not to be so." James 3:8-10.

Out of the same mouth proceed blessings and cursing, which is a sobering thought, revealing to us just how much power the tongue has. James tells us this should not be so. However, unfortunately, it also happens among Christians. The tongue should not be used to light destructive fires but to ignite faith. A good report has the same effect.

If you want your words to impact your life and others, watch what you say and how you say it!

Chapter 9

You can be strong and courageous

What does it mean to be strong and courageous? It means never to give up. Winston Churchill is quoted as saying, "Success is not final, failure is not fatal: it is the courage to continue that counts."

There is no manual we can study to know how to be strong and courageous. It is one of those mysteries that come to the fore when we face extreme danger, revealing how bravely we will react. When it comes to being strong and courageous, Christians should consider the God factor, which we will explain later.

I have a copy of the book "They Dared Mightily," which records how every Australian won the "Victoria Cross," a bravery medal awarded in battle equivalent to the American "Purple Heart." In nearly every case, they demonstrated courage while facing the enemy under fire. They never gave up or surrendered and were commended for their bravery.

I will randomly share one extract from the book that recounts how Lieutenant William John Symons won his Victoria Cross at the Gallipoli Peninsula in Turkey. On the night of 8-9 August 1915, Symonds was in charge of a section of the newly captured trenches held by his battalion and repelled several counterattacks with great coolness. The Turks made a series of determined attacks on an isolated sap (a shallow trench off the main one). Six officers were in succession killed or severely wounded in the sap, and a portion of it was lost. Symonds organised and led the charge that drove the Turks out. He killed two of the enemy with his revolver and built a wooden barricade. The Turks persisted and set fire to the barricade. Symonds led rushes against the enemy, drove them back, and extinguished the fire. Eventually, the Turks abandoned their attempt to take the sap.

Symonds survived Gallipoli, fought in France toward the end of the war, and eventually returned to Australia for a short time before settling in England, where he became a lieutenant colonel of the Home Guard during the 1939-45 war and was given command of a Battalion.

After he died in 1948, his widow put his Victoria Cross and other service medals up for auction in 1967, which a medal dealer purchased for the equivalent of $1600. The Australian Returned Servicemen's League (RSL) organised a successful fundraising appeal to buy them. The medals were eventually donated to the Australian War Memorial, where they are displayed in the Hall of Valour.

Being strong and courageous inspires others to be brave. It is reported that the Duke of Wellington said of Napoleon regarding the battle of Waterloo, "That his presence on the battlefield was worth 40,000 men." It was due to his strategic expertise, his strength, courage, and the way he inspired his men.

Consider the God Factor

We never know how someone will react in battle, but from a Christian perspective, the God Factor makes all the difference. When God prepared Joshua to lead the people into the Promised Land, what did He say to him? "Spend more time in the Gym and build up your strength so others will look at your muscles and want to follow you." No, God said to Joshua, *"Have I not commanded you? Be strong and of good courage; do not be afraid, nor be dismayed, for the Lord your God is with you wherever you go."* Joshua 1:9. This is not a choice for Joshua; it is a command. He was to be strong and courageous because he would not be alone. God promised to be **with** him wherever he went when they entered the promised land. God being with him was the God Factor. There were enemies in the promised land, giants and walled cities, that they were going to have to face and overcome. To accomplish this, they needed to be strong, courageous, and not intimidated by their enemies.

You need to be strong and courageous to lead a church and preach the gospel today. A good habit to cultivate is to remind yourself before leading or preaching, "Jesus is **with** me as I step out in faith, and He has all power and authority over my enemies."

Moses was already preparing Joshua and the people before he died. *"The Lord your God Himself crosses over before you; He will destroy those nations from before you, and you shall dispossess them. Joshua himself crosses over before you, just as the Lord has said."* …. *"Be strong and of good courage, do not fear or be afraid of them; for the Lord your God He is the One who goes with you. He will not leave you or forsake you."* Deuteronomy 31:1-6.

Moses had handed the baton over to Joshua, and the people were behind him, but the Lord also told him he had to be strong and courageous before the people to lead them to victory.

Another example we should also consider is the God Factor in David's slaying of Goliath. When it came to physical strength and experience in warfare, David was no match for the giant Goliath, but God was **with** him. *"David said to the Philistine, "You come to me with a sword, with a spear, and a Javelin. But I come to you in the name of the Lord of hosts, the God of the armies of Israel, whom you have defied. This day the Lord will deliver you into my hand."* 1 Samuel 17:45-46.

We also see the God Factor come into effect when David commissioned his son Solomon to build the temple, *"Be strong and of good courage, and do it; do not fear or be dismayed, for* **the Lord God—my God—will be with you**. *He will not leave or forsake you until you have finished all the work for the service of the house of the Lord."* 1 Chronicles 28:20. These words are almost identical to what Moses and the Lord had told Joshua.

The early church apostles set the example for Christians today. God was **with** them through the power of the Holy

Spirit, enabling them to be strong and courageous.

When Peter and John went up to the temple to pray, a man was lying there begging who had been lame since birth. They said to the man, *"Look at us." So, he gave them his attention, expecting to receive something from them. Then Peter said, "Silver and gold I do not have, but what I do have I give you: In the name of Jesus Christ of Nazareth, rise up and walk." And he took him by the right hand and lifted him up, and immediately his feet and ankle bones received strength. So, he leaping up, stood and walked and entered the temple with them, walking, and leaping and praising God."* Acts 3:4-8.

The rulers, leaders, and elders were looking for an excuse to accuse them of something, but could find none because of the evidence of this man, whom they all knew had been healed and was standing before them. But what they did observe was that, *"When they saw the boldness of Peter and John and perceived that they were uneducated and untrained men, they marvelled, and they realised that they had been with Jesus."* Acts 4:13. They knew they were fishermen and had little to offer theologically, being uneducated and untrained, but realised that their courage and boldness came from spending time with Jesus. We can surely all learn something from this about being bold.

What about the average Christian today?

You may be thinking, "Well, those leaders had to be strong and courageous to do the things they did. However, I'm not called to be a leader; I'm your average Christian, happy to attend church on Sundays. I have to work from nine to five in a regular job to earn a wage that pays the mortgage, bills, and provides food for my family, while also making a living." But that should not stop us from being strong and courageous!

I have a personally signed copy of the book *Daring to Live on the Edge* by Loren Cunningham, founder of "Youth with a Mission." In it, he has a chapter on "Living by Faith in the 9-to-5 World." He states that the average Christian seems to think the church and the mission field are places where things happen, separate from the workplace, where nothing sacred occurs, and that work is merely a place to earn wages to survive. Let me quote an excerpt from his book that refutes the 9-to-5 syndrome.

"Miracles can happen on the mission field of your regular job. God is anxious to intervene and help you in your work. If you love Jesus and are serving Him at the place where you are and in the way He has called you, you can live by faith and see spiritual victories in a factory, law office, or department store."

Dolly Parton, in her song "9 to 5", expresses the attitude many people have toward their work. It is all about working 9 to 5 to make a living.

The song may seem true for some, but as Christians, we need to adjust our attitude, make the most of our workplace, and seek opportunities to witness.

You may face obstacles in your workplace, but no matter how difficult it may seem, remember greater is He who is in you than he who is in the workplace.

"You are of God, little children, and have overcome them because He who is in you is greater than he who is in the world." 1John 4:4.

Therefore, you have every right to be strong, courageous, and have a positive voice in today's sometimes hostile world. For God is with you.

YOUR THOUGHTS SHAPE YOUR LIFE

Chapter 10

Be graciously optimistic about the future

Some people struggle to be both gracious and optimistic. Your image of an overly enthusiastic, optimistic, positive person may be that of a prideful, self-exaggerating braggart who bulldozes through life, always blaming others instead of taking responsibility for their mistakes, thereby remaining the top dog. This is not being optimistic and gracious. This kind of person has the potential to become a dangerous dictator who will not listen to anyone but themselves. They are certainly not gracious toward others.

We need enthusiastic, optimistic church leaders; however, if this type of leadership is arrogant and inconsiderate of others, it can become a problem. We are warned about avoiding this type of domineering leader in the church.

"I wrote to the church about Diotrephes, who loves to have the preeminence among them, does not receive us. Therefore, if I come, I will

call to mind his deeds which he does, prating against us with malicious words. And not content with that, he himself does not receive the brethren, and forbids those who wish to, putting them out of the church." 1 John 3:9-10.

It does not matter how optimistic a church leader may seem; they disqualify themselves by being inconsiderate, independent, and a law unto themselves. Being optimistic and gracious at the same time means treating people with dignity, honour, and respect, even when they fail or make mistakes. It is essential to respond with kindness rather than harshness while maintaining an optimistic outlook on life. To promote positive thinking effectively, we must do so without being rude, arrogant, or bombastic.

Speaking with authority

Jesus' words were both gracious and authoritative. *"They marvelled at the gracious words that proceeded out of His mouth."* …. *"And they were astonished at His teaching, for His words were with authority."* Luke 4:22 and v32. Jesus somehow struck the perfect balance of grace and truth. We need to do the same. Being gracious does not mean we become weak and wishy-washy, nor does it mean speaking with authority; it does not mean we become dictatorial and bombastic. Speaking with authority is speaking on behalf of God, proclaiming His word with conviction and inspiration, without condemnation.

Positive optimism from a Christian perspective involves expecting good things, even in challenging times. It means having a positive outlook on life, even in the face of uncertainty. Optimistic people believe that things will ultimately turn out well, based on scriptures like *"We know that all things work together for good to those who love God, to those who are called to His purpose."* Romans 8:28. It does not mean that everything that happens is good, but that God is working things out for our good. This is not only applicable to leaders but to all Christians who should be gracious, loving and considerate of one another. *"Let nothing be done through selfish ambition or conceit, but in lowliness of mind let each esteem others better than himself. Let each one of you look out not only for his own interests, but also for the interests of others."* Philippians 2:3-4.

However, we are not perfect; we all make mistakes, and in our enthusiasm, we may have been too harsh in judging others. But this is where we need to show grace to resolve any misunderstanding or heal the hurts we may have caused. We need to admit our mistakes, apologise, and ask for forgiveness if we have become offensive in our zeal to be optimistic.

Why love never fails

As important as it is to be positive, it is no excuse to overlook the grace of God and ignore His love. Paul reminds us in 1 Corinthians 13:8, *"Love never fails."*

He says this in the context of the supremacy of love compared to spiritual gifts, eloquence, knowledge, and even sacrifice. It would seem that some were proud and boasted of their superior spirituality through the use of spiritual gifts, knowledge, and prophecy. Paul does not condemn this but reminds them that these gifts will eventually cease when Christ returns. However, since God is love and His love is eternal, it is for this reason that His love will never fail.

In the context of church life, Paul says we can have all the gifts—prophecy, knowledge, faith—and make sacrifices, but without love, we just make a lot of noise.

Drop your stones of condemnation

When they brought the woman to Jesus, who was caught in the act of adultery according to the Jewish law, they wanted to stone her to death. They had picked up stones and were ready to stone her. Then they asked Jesus what should be done according to the law to test Him to see what He would say and do.

"So, when they continued asking Him, He raised himself up and said to them, He who is without sin among you, let him throw a stone at her first." John 8:7.

As a result, their conscience convicted them, and they dropped their stones and walked away one by one, starting with the eldest and proceeding down to the last. Jesus showed grace despite the Jewish law. Can we do the same? Jesus was optimistic about her future when He said to her, *"Neither do I condemn you; go and sin no more."* Verse 11.

This does not mean that we condone illegal or criminal activity, as defined by the law of the land.

But from a Christian perspective, grace gives us a reason to be optimistic and believe in a better outcome in our struggles through life. The law condemns and reveals sin; grace reveals a loving, forgiving Saviour.

"Moreover, the law entered that the offence might abound. But where

sin abounded, grace abounded much more, so that sin reigned in death, even so grace might reign through righteousness to eternal life through Jesus Christ our Lord." Romans 5:20-21.

Those who are strong in the faith and optimistic must not condemn or judge those who are weak in the faith (Romans 14:1-8), but rather make allowances for some of their idiosyncrasies.

Where sin abounded under the Jewish law, now grace abounds much more through Christ. His grace is more than enough. Someone will say, "But that is no excuse to keep sinning." Yes, that is correct, but if we do, we are not knocked out of the race or disqualified, because His grace enables us to seek forgiveness and bounce back again.

You are probably familiar with clichés, such as "The glass is half full or half empty." The implication is that if we say, "half full," we are optimistic, whereas saying "half empty" implies we are pessimistic. This is not a definitive guideline, but it provides a basic understanding of how we interpret the difference between optimism and pessimism. Christian optimism based on grace accepts that, in our struggles, God's grace is sufficient for us to live in victory.

Despite our difficulties, we are to move forward with life, believing that all things work out for the best. Statistics show that most of us are not naturally born optimists; however, it is a trait we can develop if we are prepared to work on it.

You can learn how to think optimistically

John Maxwell, in his book *How Successful People Think: Change*

Your Thinking Change Your Life, says, "I've studied successful people for forty years, and though the diversity you find among them is outstanding, I've found that they are all alike in one way: they have all learned how to think."

In his book L*earned Optimism*, Martin E. P. Seligman, PhD, says, "The good news is that pessimists can learn the skills of optimism and permanently improve the quality of their lives. Even the most optimistic individuals can benefit from learning how to adapt and change. Almost all optimists have periods of at least mild depression, and the techniques that benefit pessimists can be used by optimists when they are down." A good guide to learning optimism is how we view setbacks in life. The *optimist* usually sees them as temporary. The *pessimist* views them as permanent, believing they are responsible for many things.

Willie Jolley, a motivational speaker and author, wrote a book titled *"A Setback Is a Setup for a Comeback: Turn Your Moments of Doubt and Fear into Times of Triumph."* He popularised the phrase "A Setback is a Setup for a Comeback." He emphasises that a setback is not the end but a bump in the road —an opportunity for growth and ultimate triumph.

His key formula is "VDAD", which involves having a **V**ision beyond your setback, making **D**ecisions to pursue that vision, taking **A**ction in deliberate steps to achieve it, and maintaining a **D**esire to keep the motivation and process going to see it fulfilled.

Many of the great biblical heroes of faith, renowned for their exploits, bounced back after encountering setbacks.

Joseph is a good biblical example

Joseph was his father's favourite son, but his brothers were jealous and hated him. He had an optimistic dream that only fuelled more hatred. *"Now Israel loved Joseph more than all his children, because he was the son of his old age. Also, he made him a tunic of many colours. But when his brothers saw that his father loved him more than all his brothers, they hated him and could not speak peaceably to him. Now Joseph had a dream, and he told it to his brothers, and they hated him even more. So, he said to them, "Please hear this dream which I have dreamed: There we were binding sheaves in the field. Then behold, my sheaf arose and stood upright; and indeed, your sheaves stood all around and bowed down to my sheaf." And his brothers said to him, "Shall you indeed reign over us? Or shall you indeed have dominion over us?" So, they hated him even more for his dreams and for his words."* Genesis 37:3-8.

However, to make things worse, he had another dream similar to the first one. When he enthusiastically shared his dream, it was not well-received.

"Then he dreamed still another dream and told it to his brothers, and said, "Look, I have dreamed another dream. And this time, the sun, the moon, and the eleven stars bowed down to me." So, he told it to his father and his brothers, and his father rebuked him. "What is this dream you have dreamed? Shall your mother and I and your brothers indeed come and bow down to the earth to you?" And his brothers envied him, but his father kept the matter in mind." Genesis 37: 9-11. However, this did not appear to be the case, as Joseph suffered a significant setback: his brothers conspired against him and sold him to some Midianite traders. The brothers had taken his tunic, dipped it in goat's blood, and given it to his father and told him

wild beasts had torn him apart. The Midianites sold Joseph in Egypt to Potiphar, who was an officer of Pharaoh, where he became a slave. But Joseph found favour with Potiphar and became successful, being appointed the overseer of his household. Then Joseph faced another major setback when his master's wife asked him to lie with her, but he refused. However, she grabbed his garment as he fled, then she accused him of trying to seduce her, so his master had him thrown in prison.

However, over time, he gained the jailer's favour, who knew he could accurately interpret dreams. When Pharaoh had a dream that troubled him, and no one could interpret it, the jailer told Pharaoh about Joseph. He was summoned to interpret the dream. He told Pharaoh that the dream meant there would be seven years of good harvests followed by seven years of famine, and that he should prepare for the famine during the years of plenty. Pharaoh was pleased with Joseph, and as a result, he was promoted to ruler over all of Egypt and was tasked with preparing for the years of drought. Despite his setbacks, we can see that they became a setup for a comeback. During the seven years of famine, his brothers came seeking food from Egypt and bowed down to him, just as he had seen in his dream he had shared with them many years ago. Joseph had learned to be optimistic about the future because he knew his dream was from God. He also showed amazing grace to his brothers who had sold him into slavery, and was eventually reconciled to them, and once again he was able to see his father. We observe that justice is often a process that unfolds over time; it is not always immediate. It is up to us to remain optimistic in the meantime.

Be graciously optimistic about the future

Nelson Mandela spent twenty-seven years in a South African prison, suffering because of the apartheid regime. He refused to become bitter and emerged with a message of forgiveness and reconciliation. He eventually became the first black president of South Africa. He is quoted as saying, "I am fundamentally an optimist. Whether that comes from nature or nurture, I cannot say." He changed the course of history for that nation.

I encourage you to remain optimistic. Your setback may be an opportunity to make a comeback and change your world.

YOUR THOUGHTS SHAPE YOUR LIFE

Chapter 11

Your vision must have a purpose

You need to ask yourself a few leading questions, such as, "Why am I here?" What is my vision and purpose in life? What gives me a spark that ignites a fire in my belly? What gives me something to live or die for? What motivates me to speak positively and set goals to reach my objectives?

US President Woodrow Wilson asserted, "You are not here merely to make a living. You are here to enable the world to live more amply, with greater vision, with a finer spirit of hope and achievement. You are here to enrich the world, and to impoverish yourself if you forget the errand."

Once you have a vision, do not focus on the obstacles that seem to stand in the way. Continue pursuing your vision, as it will inspire a positive outlook on life. Others will tell you why it can't be done. If God tells you to do something, He will enable you to do it and see it through to completion.

Your vision may depend on your calling in life. This does not mean we all have to conjure up some grandiose vision to set the world on fire. If you asked my wife, she would probably say that her vision when she was working was to be a successful teacher. Now, in retirement, she is a wonderful wife, mother, and grandmother, as well as a support to her husband and family.

The first book I wrote, *Unlocking Your Purpose*, explores the "Keys to Discovering Your God-Given Purpose and How to Pursue It." Once you discover your God-given purpose, it enables you to develop a positive mindset and work out a plan of action.

"Write the vision and make it plain on tablets, that he may run who reads it." Habakkuk 2:2-3. Writing down your vision gives you something to memorise, visualise, meditate on, be positive about, and aim at in life.

Avoid living an aimless life

It is reputed that the great Greek Philosopher Aristotle once said, "Our problem is NOT that we aim too high and miss. Our problem is that we aim too low and hit." We often avoid bold dreams and visions because of the disappointment of failing to reach those goals. Instead, we settle for something quiet and safe or, worse still, nothing at all.

Without a purpose, life becomes aimless, and we are more likely to develop a negative outlook. If your vision is to succeed in your work or business and to help support a church or mission, then this could be your God-given purpose in life. Having a vision is better than having no vision at all.

Life needs to have a purpose; otherwise, there seems to be no reason for our existence.

Solomon implies throughout Ecclesiastes that life is futile unless it has a purpose. *"Vanity of vanities, says the preacher; all is vanity." What profit has a man from all his labour in which he toils under the sun? One generation passes away, and another generation comes."* Ecclesiastes 1:2-3. What he is getting at is that life has no real meaning or purpose without God. He describes life without God as shallow, empty, and meaningless, emphasising the need to be connected to a God-given purpose.

At the end of the book, he concludes with this simple but profound statement, *"Fear God and keep His commandments, for this is man's whole duty (purpose)."* Ecclesiastes 12:13.

A healthy fear of God

Jesus said, *"Do not fear those who kill the body but cannot kill the soul. But rather fear Him who is able to destroy both soul and body in hell."* Matthew 10:28.

Jonathan Edwards, an 18th-century preacher, is quoted in his famous sermon, "Sinners in the Hands of an Angry God," as saying, "We need to dangle sinners over the flames of hell." He said this to awaken people to the reality of the gospel and their need to turn to Christ.

We need a blend of conviction, optimistic hope, and grace that brings joy to those who are struggling to live in victory. John Wesley stated, "Before I preach love, mercy and grace, I must preach law, sin and judgment." He felt that without doing this, there would be no conviction to convince the sinner of his need for Christ for salvation.

Some say this kind of preaching is unacceptable today. However, although I am a strong proponent of grace, I believe a holy fear of God is sometimes lacking in the proclamation of the gospel today.

Adapting to a progressive vision

As we go through life, we realise that our vision and purpose change as we age. Are we flexible enough to adapt to the changes that come along the way?

"Where there is no vision (prophetic vision), the people cast off restraint (perish): but happy is he who keeps the law." Proverbs 29:18.

For Christians, "Keeping His law" does not mean trying to keep the Jewish Law and traditions in a legalistic manner; today, under the new covenant, it means simply following Christ and His teachings. Jesus said to Simon and Andrew, his brother, who were fishermen, *"Come after Me and I will make you fishers of men."* Mark 1:16-17. He was giving them a God-given purpose, not to catch fish, but to catch men by becoming disciples of Jesus and preachers of the gospel.

Vision is always progressive. Until I retired, my vision was to pastor, teach, and preach the Word of God. When I retired from pastoring a church, I still maintained a God-given purpose. I preached in a few other churches, lectured regularly at a Bible School, and went on ministry trips mainly to PNG, where I had established a Bible College and ministered throughout the mission field. Today, I still mentor a few pastors.

In recent years, I have been busy writing inspirational books and thoroughly enjoying the process. This will be my eighth book. My seventh, "Do Angels Walk Among Us Today?" This will have been published by the time you read this.

Abraham is called the father of our faith. God gave him a progressive vision. *"I will make you a great nation; I will bless you and make your name great; and you shall be a blessing."* Genesis 12:2. Again, we read that this vision would be a legacy for generations to come. *"Then he brought him outside and said, "Look now toward heaven, and count the stars if you are able to number them." And He said to him, So, shall your descendants be." And he believed in the Lord, and He accounted it to him for righteousness."* Genesis 15:5-6.

God's timing is always right

Although Abraham was given a great vision, he and Sarah became desperate because they were well past childbearing age and still had no son. So, Sarah sent Abraham to their servant, Hagar, to bear a child for them. Like Abraham and Sarah, we may at times take things into our own hands, thinking we are helping God. However, when we have done something wrong, we must repent and move forward, reassess our priorities, and refocus on God's purpose and plan for our lives. Despite taking matters into their own hands to try to make it happen, Abraham still maintained his faith in God for a son, as God had promised.

"And not being weak in faith, he did not consider his own body, already dead (since he was about one hundred years old), and the deadness of Sarah's womb. He did not waver at the promise of God through unbelief

but was strengthened in faith, giving glory to God, and being fully convinced that what He had promised He was also able to perform. And therefore, it was accounted to him as righteousness." Romans 4:19-22.

Modern-day possibility thinkers

There have been many "possibility thinkers" who have accomplished great things in our lifetime. Walt Disney was a possibility thinker with a purpose. His purpose was to entertain people by bringing joy and imagination to life. He created "Disneyland" despite much ridicule and opposition. As a result, he established one of the most iconic and beloved entertainment empires in history.

Elon Musk has pioneered and popularised electric cars through his Tesla empire. He has a vision to colonise Mars. His purpose is to make interplanetary space travel possible. SpaceX has developed a reusable rocket and is working toward this goal. He is a controversial figure, with both supporters and opponents of his plans.

"Possibility thinkers" appear to share these familiar traits. *Firstly*, they have a clear and compelling purpose. *Secondly*, a refusal to accept "impossible' as a final answer. *Thirdly*, an inspired vision with a conviction of faith and hope for a better future.

A purpose-driven church

In his book *The Purpose-Driven Church*, Rick Warren says, "The starting point for every church should be the question, 'Why do we exist?" We could ask ourselves the same question as individuals. At the heart of his book is the belief that churches grow healthier, not just larger, when they are driven by "purpose" rather than programs, personalities, or traditions. Rick Warren, building on the success of his Saddleback Church in California, which we visited some years ago, outlines five core purposes that he believes the church should be built around.

1. Worship - Loving God with all our heart.
2. Ministry - Loving your neighbour as yourself.
3. Evangelism - Going and making disciples.
4. Fellowship - Baptising them. (the Body of Christ).
5. Discipleship - Teaching them to obey Christ.

He believes a healthy church balances all five of these and structures strategies around them.

Jesus is building His church

The church is an ongoing work in progress. Despite centuries of opposition, the church remains steadfast in its purpose to proclaim the gospel of the Kingdom of God to the world. This task is not easy, but the church is equipped to overcome any obstacle the devil will put in its way.

Jesus, the most significant possibility thinker of all time, said, *"I will build My church, and the gates of Hades will not prevail against it."* Matthew 16:18.

The church may not be perfect, but it does not matter what is thrown at the church by the gates of Hades; the church will overcome and prevail. The death, burial, and resurrection of Jesus ensure us of this victory.

Possibility thinkers are united by an unwavering vision and purpose, enabling them to overcome obstacles and opposition. Their goals are clear and often larger than themselves, with a vision for a better future. They push through difficulties and will sometimes use them as fuel for innovation. Their vision and purpose inspire them and others to strive for a significant difference in their world. You too can make a difference!

Chapter 12

Be inspired by Godly affirmations

We all like to have someone who means a lot to us, who affirm us by patting us on the back, hugging us, and saying something like, "Well done." "I appreciate you and what you did; you are a real blessing."

When God calls someone to serve Him, He usually gives them the affirmation they need to develop a positive outlook, ignite their faith, and inspire them to fulfil their mission. Jesus was baptised by John the Baptist in the river Jordan. God the Father affirmed that Jesus was His Son when He came out of the water. *"When He had been baptised, Jesus came up immediately from the water; and behold, the heavens were opened to Him, and He saw the Spirit of God descending like a dove and alighting on Him. And suddenly a voice came from heaven, saying, "This is My beloved Son, in whom I am well pleased."* Matthew 3:16-17.

God the Father was affirming Jesus as His Son for all to

hear and see. We loved to be affirmed by our parents. We also see affirmation from the Holy Spirit, who descended on Jesus as a dove. Jesus affirmed His disciples when Andrew brought his brother Simon to Jesus, declaring, *"We have found the Messiah," which is translated, the Christ." Jesus said to him, "You are Simon, the son of Jonah, you shall be called Cephas" (which is translated as "a stone").* John 1:42.

Jesus was giving Peter affirmation by changing his name from Simon (meaning a reed) to Peter, which means a stone or a rock. Jesus saw the hidden potential in Peter, just like He sees it in you. God has many ways of affirming you, through His Word, the laying on of hands, prophecy, friends, those in ministry, visions, and dreams. It is usually in the context of church fellowship, but may also arise through casual conversation. I will elaborate on some of these.

Affirmation through the laying on of hands

On several occasions, the apostle Paul encouraged Timothy, his son in the faith, by affirming what God had imparted to him through the laying on of hands. *"Therefore, I remind you to stir up the gift of God which is in you through the laying on of my hands. For God has not given us a spirit of fear, but of power, love and of a sound mind."* 2 Timothy 1:6-7.

There can be an impartation by the laying on of hands, but it is hard to explain because it is a work of the Spirit. Paul implies that Timothy received a gift by the laying on of his hands. This was an affirmation that Timothy needed to recall to confirm his ministry. He must have been facing some fears regarding the ministry, Paul says, "You have not received a spirit of fear, so stir up this gift."

Jesus laid hands on people, mainly to impart healing. The apostles did the same. Laying hands on people in the early church was a sign of affirmation of their ministry. When they had set aside seven men for ministry, the apostles laid hands on them and prayed. (Acts 6:6). Peter and John laid hands on Samaritan believers, and they received the Holy Spirit. (Acts 8:17).

Affirmation through prophecy

The laying on of hands, often accompanied by prophecy, was a source of affirmation that strengthened faith and deepened a spiritual connection.

When Paul and Barnabas were in Antioch, they had fasted, prayed, prophesied, and laid hands on them to send them off as missionaries. (Acts 13:1-3). Paul reminded Timothy to use prophecies made over him as a weapon in spiritual warfare.

"This charge I commit to you, son Timothy, according to the prophecies previously made concerning you, that by them you may wage the good warfare." 1 Timothy 1:18.

I have had many credible ministries lay hands on me and prophecy throughout my years in ministry, some of which I have written down. Occasionally, when I need encouragement and affirmation, especially in the face of opposition, I find myself rereading them. They strengthen my faith and help me stay positive, enabling me to overcome negative thoughts and emotions.

Affirmation through His word

Jesus likened bread to the word of God, which is our spiritual food. *"It is written: Man shall not live by bread alone, but by every word that proceeds from the mouth of God."* Matthew 4:4.

When we struggle with thoughts that hinder positive thinking, it is helpful to get into the habit of affirming the truth of God's word daily. Jesus said that when we pray, we should ask for daily bread, as in the phrase, *"Give us this day our daily bread."* Matthew 6:11. This could refer to both natural and spiritual food. We need daily bread to sustain us and strengthen us. God fed the children of Israel in the wilderness with Manna from heaven. Moses told them to gather it daily to keep it fresh.

Jesus clarifies that He is the true bread that came down from heaven. *"Moses did not give you the bread from heaven, but My Father gives you the true bread from heaven. For the bread of God is He who comes down from heaven and gives life to the world."* They said to Him, *"Lord, give us this bread always."* And Jesus said to them, *"I am the bread of life. He who comes to Me will never hunger, and he who believes in Me shall never thirst."* John 6:32-35.

Learning scriptural verses by heart or writing them down is a beneficial practice for cultivating a positive mindset. Pray over them, let them enter your heart and mind, meditate on them, and speak them aloud or to yourself, like some of the following -

* I am a child of God (John 1:12).

* I am fearfully and wonderfully made (Psalm 149:14).

* I can do all things through Christ (Philippians 4:13).

* God will never leave or forsake me (Hebrews 13:5).

* The Lord is my Shepherd: I shall not want (Psalm 23:1).

The above are just a few examples; you can use them as daily affirmations to cultivate positive thinking. Allow the Holy Spirit to lead and guide you. By doing this, you are speaking life into your situation, not death. It is good to begin the day by saying the word out loud during your devotions.

You may find it helpful to look in the mirror and speak the truth to yourself, or post scriptures in places where you will see them, to remind you of who you are and what you can accomplish in Christ.

We have two small wall plaques in our house. *"My God shall supply all your needs according to His riches in Christ Jesus."* Philippians 4:19, and the other one is *"Greater is He who is in you, than he that is in the world."* 1 John 4:4. They remind us of God's goodness and greatness.

Affirmation by family and friends

There is no greater thrill than to have your family and friends affirm you. I have been fortunate enough to have my wife, children, and friends affirm their appreciation and love for me. It does wonders for your self-esteem and helps you have a positive outlook on life.

At the risk of appearing conceited, I would like to share a couple of Facebook posts my eldest daughter, Amanda, and my youngest daughter, Sharon, posted about me to help me

YOUR THOUGHTS SHAPE YOUR LIFE

celebrate a recent significant birthday.

Amanda posted: "I am so blessed to have experienced the love of a gentle, faithful, God-honouring father. His life is a testament to quiet strength and unwavering devotion – whether he's writing another book to encourage others, swinging a golf club, treating his grandchildren, painting an Aussie landscape, cooking for mum and himself or feeding the warbling magpies. You can always count on my dad – what a gift you are to all of us. Love Amanda."

Sharon, our youngest daughter, for the same occasion, posted: "Thank you for your wisdom and all the memories I have, especially your favourite sayings: 'You're just here for the ride, kid,' 'How do you eat an elephant?' 'One bite, at a time!' When I complained and said, "You can't tell a man anything," and you said, "You sure got that right." Things I have learnt from you: Slow down a bit more. You need a good laugh. Have lots of interests. Your family is your priority. Everyone has something valuable to say, and it's about applying faith in God without being weird about it. My most cherished memories are your humour and the way you make me laugh, and laugh even when I get annoyed with something. The way you treat all of us — kids and grandkids — is the same: with love and interest. However, I'm definitely your favourite! Love Sharon.

At the same birthday party, my other daughter, Felicity and my son, Andrew, said some lovely things. It is so nice to have these things said before your funeral.

Value your relationship with those who affirm you, and

be ready to affirm yourself and others with loving, Godly affirmations that can make a difference.

How to affirm someone

You may be wondering how to affirm someone. What can you say? Here are some practical guidelines.

Affirm their Character – "I admire your integrity and your honesty." "I love your openness; you always make people feel welcome and loved."

Affirm their Effort – "Your work ethic is an example to everyone." "I admire your energy and dedication."

Affirm their impact – "You have had a profound impact on my life." Your support has changed my life."

Affirm their presence – "Your presence makes a huge difference to me and everyone else." "Things would not be so good without your presence."

Affirm their progress – "You have come a long way in such a short time." "The way you have grown and gained confidence is amazing."

You may think of other ways to affirm people. You may want to give them a positive word from the Lord, a prophecy or an appropriate scripture as an affirmation.

Whatever you do, make sure that the Holy Spirit is leading you to do it.

YOUR THOUGHTS SHAPE YOUR LIFE

Chapter 13

Do not neglect the marginalised

The phrase *"Imago Dei" (Latin for "Image of God")* is a theological concept that posits every person is created in the image of God (Genesis 1:27) and is of intrinsic value, regardless of one's social status, race, culture, or religion.

However, the marginalised are often overlooked as being of lesser value. So, whatever your vision may be, you need to ask yourself, does it include the marginalised that we sometimes are inclined to neglect?

In Australia, many of us seem to be better off than we were years ago. I recall that, as a boy, being a millionaire was something to aspire to. These days, if you are fortunate enough to own your own house, it is probably worth around a million dollars. So, asset-wise, you are a millionaire. However, we also have those who are less fortunate, including renters and the homeless, who struggle to make ends meet.

In his book Sins of the *Filthy Rich: Tales of Wicked Wealth*, Dr Peter Coleman examines the seven deadly sins—envy, gluttony, sloth, lust, pride, wrath, and greed — as committed on an epic scale by ultra-wealthy figures throughout history. Although he acknowledges the generosity and charity of others, he highlights how extreme wealth often leads to social harm, a lack of accountability, and the power to change the world. Yet, they are so obsessed with accumulating wealth for themselves that they seem to forget about others who need it most.

If you lead a church, your vision may involve attracting good, influential, and successful people because you need their support and value their contributions. They are possibility thinkers who can contribute to your vision. But does your vision neglect the marginalised? If it does, you are missing the heart of Christianity.

We will use, as an example, the lawyer who, in response to the command to love God and your neighbour, asks Jesus, "Who is your neighbour?" To answer him, Jesus tells a story about a certain man who went down from Jerusalem to Jericho and fell among thieves who stripped him of his clothing, wounded him, and left him half dead. Jesus points out that a priest saw him and crossed to the other side of the road to avoid him, and then a Levite saw him and did the same. However, a certain Samaritan saw him and had compassion on him, bandaged his wounds, took him to an inn, and paid money so they would take care of him. Jesus said to the lawyer, *"Which of these three was a neighbour to him who fell among the thieves?" And he said, "He who showed mercy on him." Then Jesus said to him, "Go and do likewise."* (Luke 10:25-37).

Compassion begins by seeing and recognising a need. The point is that the ones who should have been compassionate, the Priest and the Levite, saw the need and deliberately looked the other way and avoided this man who had become a victim of robbers and was left to die. This could be indicative of Christians or churches who see the need but show no compassion, ignoring those who need help, which also includes the marginalised.

Who then are the marginalised?

They are usually individuals or groups who are pushed to the edge of society and denied the rights, opportunities, and resources available to others.

For example, to mention a few, this may include the poor and needy, the homeless, racial and ethnic minorities, indigenous communities and refugees, people with disabilities, the frail and the elderly, women and girls who are denied equal rights, education, and opportunities, and the unemployed with no stable income. *"Whoever oppresses the poor shows contempt for their maker, but whoever is kind to the needy honours God."* Proverbs 14:31 (NIV).

God expects us to minister to the marginalised and not to discard them as dysfunctional members of society.

According to the 2021 Census in Australia, there were just over half a million single-parent families with a dependent child under fifteen years of age, and just over 1.5 million people living in single-parent families. The vast majority of single parents are women. Single-parent families experience much higher rates of poverty. "Fatherlessness" is a growing problem in Australia and the Western world, whether caused by divorce, broken families, or single parenting; more and more children are growing up without fathers.

Jesus came to preach the gospel to all. But the scripture is clear: when we examine an outline of His ministry, as in the scripture below, the marginalised were very much on His mind. *"The Spirit of the Lord is upon Me. Because He has anointed Me to preach the gospel to the poor, He has sent Me to heal the brokenhearted, to proclaim liberty to the captives and recovery of sight to the blind, to set at liberty those who are oppressed: to proclaim the acceptable year of the Lord."* Luke 4:18-19.

These verses depict marginalised people, desperate and in need of help. Jesus said that God anointed him to minister to them. This does not mean we are limited to only ministering to those on this list. Every person is valuable to God, whether poor or rich, healthy or unhealthy, stable or unstable, mentally sound or unsound; all need to hear the gospel.

However, we need to realise that some people do not want to change for fear of the unknown. There was a certain man who had an infirmity for thirty-eight years, lying at the pool of Bethesda, waiting for an angel to come and stir the waters so he could be healed. When Jesus saw him, he said, *"Do you want to be made well?"* John 5:6. You would think the answer would be obvious. Jesus must have discerned that he had faith to be healed because he told him to rise, take up his bed, and walk, so he did. But sometimes, people, despite their infirmity, get used to their lifestyle and want to be left alone. They choose the certainty of misery rather than the misery of uncertainty. Some will choose the misery they know and experience over the uncertainty of what change may bring to their lifestyle. Some are afraid of losing their government benefits and being forced to look for a better job to support themselves if they are healed. Others may choose a lifestyle of living in sin and totally reject the gospel. But we should always give them the benefit of the doubt.

See the value of the person, not the label

Sometimes we are quick to judge people and assign labels. They may have chronic disorders like autism, be diagnosed as bipolar, or be mentally or physically disabled in some way. However, they should not be overlooked and put in the 'too-hard' basket. We need to love them, and if we cannot help, they may require professional assistance.

Many years ago, Chuck Girard sang a song called "Don't Shoot the Wounded." The lyrics went like this –

> "Don't shoot the wounded; they need us more than ever
> They need our love, no matter what it is they've done
> Sometimes we just condemn them,
> And don't take time to hear their story
> Don't shoot the wounded, someday you might be one."

Wounded people (who are often marginalised) are frequently desperate and need help; they should be loved, cared for, and nurtured back to health. Sometimes we unintentionally write them off, thinking they are beyond help. But the hidden message of the song is "Don't shoot the wounded, someday you might be one." We do not know the future; it only takes a bad accident, and we may become one of the wounded.

Hospitals have intensive care units to cater for those with serious medical issues. What about the church from a spiritual perspective? Wounded people need more than "You haven't got enough faith or "Be more positive." Those who have been through trauma, grief, loss, or hardships need time to recover.

Caring for others does not mean we ignore our family and neglect the responsibility we have toward them. I have been guilty of this at times.

My wife and family have always been important to me, and so has my calling and vision to serve the Lord. It's a juggling act at times as I strive for a balanced lifestyle that accommodates both my family and my vision.

Value family and friendships

We all face the challenge of prioritising the day-to-day responsibilities and necessities we need to survive, while also spending quality time with our family and friends. How many people on their deathbeds wished they had spent more time in the office?

Most people wish they had spent more time with family and friends. These are to be valued. They are relationships that last through all seasons. Most of our personal friendships have been related to those in ministry. However, we also value some friendships we have tried to maintain with those who are, in my opinion, marginalised or have some form of disability. We all need each other. *"A friend loves at all times, and a brother is born for a time of adversity."* Proverbs 17:17 (NIV).

Good friends stick by you in times of hardship, pain and suffering. Just like God, they never forsake you.

There is an old Country and Western song by Alan Jackson that I identify with as I grow older. Some of the lyrics go like this-

"The older I get, the fewer friends I have,

But you don't need a lot when the ones that you got have always got your back."

Christians are never left alone

You may experience loneliness, but no one is left alone, including the marginalised. I have just watched a television series called "Alone Australia", in which about 12 people were placed around a lake in the remote, rugged bushland of Tasmania. They were alone, had to build their shelter, live off the land, and survive in cold, wet weather. The last one to survive the longest won $250,000. One of the contestants was a man with a disability who used a hook-like device as an artificial hand. I was amazed at what he could do and how long he lasted before having to withdraw. However, I noticed something as they dropped out one by one. They began to think negatively about their situation. Loneliness got the better of them, and they missed their family. Shay Williamson eventually won it. He maintained a positive attitude and was the last one standing after 76 days.

You might be saying to me, "You do not understand, I am all alone." "I have no partner," or "Mine is deceased," "I am single," "I am divorced," or "I have no immediate family to help me." "I can barely survive, let alone pursue a vision." Yes, you may be lonely, but let me remind you that, as a Christian, you are never left alone. God also sets the lonely (including the marginalised) in families —if not physically, then certainly spiritually, by placing us in a church family. *"God is a Father to the fatherless, a defender of widows, is God in His Holy habitation. God sets the solitary in families. He brings out those who are bound into prosperity."* Psalm 68:5-6. For those who are lonely, there are many benefits of belonging to a church.

Chapter 14

Avoid going into panic mode

You need to avoid going into panic mode when you are suddenly confronted with an unexpected fear. You need to take stock of the situation and think clearly, rather than panic. Your decisions made under pressure in the fog of battle may not always be the right ones.

When I was pastoring in Lismore, we once had three brilliant Christian doctors in the church. One of them was the late Dr Fiona Wagner. She was a very dedicated Christian, married to Stephen, a farmer.

I was planning a ministry trip to Hyderabad, India. I had arranged with Dr Wagner to undergo a medical checkup and receive the recommended vaccinations as a preventive measure against certain diseases.

During the consultation, she warned me that the injections could be painful. Then she suddenly confronted me with this enormous syringe. When it looked as though I was about to pass out, she apologised and said her husband had put her up to it. The syringe was one he used for cattle on their farm.

What a relief! The point is, I was suddenly surprised by an unexpected fear that took control of my thoughts instead of faith. I jumped to conclusions, and my thoughts became exceedingly pessimistic about the possible outcome. But as soon as I realised there was no longer any danger, I regained my composure and faith.

How should we react?

When confronted with a sudden fear or an unexpected event, our bodies and brains enter a heightened state of stress, known as the fight-or-flight response. As the term suggests, some will fight to survive, while others will withdraw or flee. We all react differently; if we panic, our reasoning and decision-making process may become confused, leading to incorrect decisions.

In 2009, an Airline pilot, Captain "Sully" Sullenberger, calmly landed his plane on the Hudson River after both engines had failed due to a bird strike. Instead of going into panic mode, he remained focused and followed his training for such an event. The airline remained afloat long enough for everyone to be rescued.

When I retired from pastoring, I became a Volunteer with the Volunteer Marine Rescue (VMR) organisation, which rescues people in trouble on the water. We had to learn how to drive the rescue boats in sometimes hazardous conditions. We also learned to steer and control the boat in difficult situations without using the steering wheel by adjusting the twin-motor sticks. This was not easy, as it depended on the wind and the tide.

If we were suddenly confronted with unexpected danger, such as a possible collision, a sandbar, or underwater rocks, we were trained not to panic. We are more likely to experience an adrenaline rush and overreact, which can worsen the situation. It may lead to a wrong decision and put everyone in danger.

The key was to slow down, think it through, and say to yourself, "I've got this, I can handle this, I am in control." Then act quickly if necessary. Of course, this is easier said than done when lives are put at risk. We all face the challenge of overcoming hindrances to positive thinking. Therefore, we need to identify the hindrances most likely to affect us and learn to manage them. From a Christian perspective, we need to remember that God is in control. Sometimes, when we face severe adversity, we often wonder where God is, thinking He has forsaken us. The disciples felt like this when their boat was caught in a storm. They went into panic mode.

"A great windstorm arose, and the waves beat into the boat, so that it was already filling. But He (Jesus) was in the stern asleep on a pillow. And they awoke him and said to Him, "Teacher, do you not care that we are perishing?" Then He arose and rebuked the wind, and said to the sea, "Peace be still." And the wind ceased, and there was a great calm. Mark 4:37-40. They woke Jesus, thinking they were about to perish. Jesus did not panic. He was in complete control. He spoke peace into the storm, and there was a great calm.

Do not panic under sudden adversity

Some people face sudden adverse circumstances, suffering loss and experiencing grief, that is no fault of their own, like Job in the Bible. We are told Job was a blameless and upright man, feared God and shunned evil. He had seven sons and three daughters. His possessions comprised seven thousand sheep, three thousand camels, five hundred oxen, and five hundred female donkeys.

Job had a very large household, was extremely wealthy, and was the greatest of all the people in the East. God was pleased with Job and told Satan that there was no one on earth like Job, who was blameless, upright, feared God, and shunned evil. However, Satan accused God of putting a hedge around him to protect him and his household and all his possessions.

So, Satan challenged God and said, *"But now stretch out Your hand and touch all that he has, and he will surely curse You to Your face." And the Lord said to Satan, "All that he has is in your power; only do not lay a hand on his person." So, Satan went out from the presence of the Lord."* Job 1:11-12.

Then Job was confronted with one sudden, unexpected adversity after another, and he lost everything, including all his children. When Job received news of these disasters, he had every right to imagine the worst-case scenarios, but what did he do? Did he curse God like Satan predicted?

No, he did not. "Job arose, tore his robe, and shaved his head; and he fell to the ground and worshipped. And said, *"Naked I came from my mother's womb, and naked shall I return there. The Lord gave and the Lord has taken away; Blessed be the name of the Lord." In all this, Job did not sin nor charge God with wrong."* Job 1:20-22. Despite his situation, Job refused to blame God; he continued to believe in God's goodness. However, next time Satan came before God, God basically said, "I told you so. Job still holds fast to his integrity; he did not curse Me." This provoked Satan to try again.

"So, Satan answered the Lord and said, "Skin for Skin! Yes, all that a man has will he give for his life, and he will still curse you........." And the Lord said to Satan, "Behold, he is in your hand, but spare his life." So, Satan went out from the presence of the Lord, and struck Job with painful boils from the sole of his foot to the crown of his head." Job 2:4-7.

His wife was extremely negative this time and provided no help or support. She said, *"Do you still hold fast to your integrity? Curse God and Die!" But he said to her, "You speak as one of the foolish women speaks. Shall we indeed accept good from God, and shall we not accept adversity?" In all this, Job did not sin with his lips."* Job 2:9-10.

Although his wife wanted him to forsake his integrity and to curse God and die, he maintained his integrity and faith in the goodness of God despite the adversity he was facing. What a positive attitude and confession to match his faith! Job had a belief system that enabled him to stay positive. He had to battle negative thoughts from not only his wife, but also his friends, who kept implying that he must have sinned or upset God by doing something to offend Him. But in the end, God was gracious to him, and Job ended up with twice as much as he had lost.

What about an unexpected blessing?

How do we handle a sudden blessing? We are to trust that it is from God. Before Jesus ascended, He instructed His disciples to tarry in Jerusalem, assuring them that He would send the promise of His Father upon them until they were endued with power from on high. He was referring to the outpouring of the Holy Spirit. (Luke 24:49).

The disciples had a promise from Jesus, but they had no idea what it would look like. They tarried in Jerusalem, as instructed, not knowing how this would happen. Suddenly, on the day of Pentecost, we read of this incredible historical event.

"When the day of Pentecost had fully come, they were all with one accord in one place. And suddenly there came a sound from heaven, as of a rushing mighty wind, and it filled the whole house where they were sitting. Then there appeared to them divided tongues, as of fire, and one sat on each of them. And they were all filled with the Holy Spirit and began to speak with other tongues, as the Spirit gave them utterance." Acts 2:1-4.

They were suddenly confronted with these strange events, but they remained positive, accepting this as the fulfilment of the promised Holy Spirit.

But it was not without some opposition from sceptics. *"Others mocking, said they are full of new wine."* Acts 2:13. However, Peter assured them that this was not the case, as it was only 9 a.m. Peter then preached, explaining that this was what the prophet Joel had prophesied: in the last days, God would pour out His Spirit on all flesh. (Acts 2:16-17).

Jesus wants us to believe when He promises to give us something that will benefit and bless us. He wants us to understand that He is a loving Father who will take good care of us. He says earthly fathers are evil, yet knowing how to give good gifts to their children —how much more will God?

Jesus said, *"If a son asks bread from any father among you, will you give him a stone? Or if he asks for a fish, will you give him a serpent instead of a fish? Or if he asks for an egg, will he offer him a scorpion? If you, then being evil, know how to give good gifts to your children, how much more will your heavenly Father give the Holy Spirit to those who ask Him."* Luke 11:11-13.

So, if you are in any way sceptical, Jesus is assuring you that God is not like this. God loves you and will gladly give you the Holy Spirit to bless, lead, and guide you.

No need to panic, He loves you

"There is no fear in love; but perfect love casts out fear, because fear involves torment. But he who fears has not been made perfect in love. We love Him because He first loved us." 1 John 4:18.

This assurance that God's love drives out fear in us gives us, as Christians, every right to challenge fearful, negative thoughts that threaten or torment us in some way. You should be confident and optimistic about your relationship with God. Once your belief system is firmly rooted in the love of God and His goodness toward you, you can transform your negative thoughts into positive ones by speaking words of life and blessing.

So, when you are suddenly confronted and surprised by

the unexpected, think about best-case scenarios by trusting in the promises of God.

Chapter 15

Go after the life you are hoping for

We all need hopes and dreams for the future. God wants to give you a future and a hope despite your limitations. Are you going after what God wants for your life? Do you know what that looks like? Ask God to reveal to you what it is, and then pursue it.

Nick Vujicic was born in Melbourne, Australia. His parents were shocked and devastated when he was born without limbs. Growing up, Nick struggled with immense physical and emotional challenges, including bullying, depression, and a period of hopelessness. Nick has openly shared that at age ten, he considered suicide, feeling he had no future. The turning point came when he turned to Christ and embraced his faith in God, beginning to see himself not as disabled but as uniquely equipped for a purpose.

Nick founded the organisation "Life Without Limbs,"

aiming to share the gospel and inspire people worldwide to overcome adversity. I have had the pleasure of hearing him speak at conferences, and he is truly amazing—his message centres around hope, faith and perseverance. He often quotes, *"For I know the thoughts that I think toward you, says the Lord, thoughts of peace and not of evil, to give you a future and a hope."* Jeremiah 29:11.

It is encouraging to know that God thinks positively of us, giving us a future and hope. I have often wondered why the verse puts a future before a hope. I would have thought that we need to have hope for the future. I believe the NIV is the only translation that presents it in this manner. Perhaps we should prioritise knowing our future, so our hopes have something to aim for. Maybe we need to visualise the big picture before we can hope, plan, and set goals toward it.

Be enthusiastic about what you hope for

The word "enthusiasm" originates from the Greek "en theos" (in God), so, in a sense, enthusiasm is a divine passion stemming from a connection to a Higher Power. As a Christian, you need to pursue the life you hope for with enthusiasm. It is a dynamic quality that we may not always have, but we can acquire it if we put our mind to it. You can build it into your personality and lifestyle through practising it.

Enthusiasm rubs off on others and inspires them to follow your example. We see it influencing all areas of life, whether in the church, business, sports, the music industry, or the arts and theatre.

Your enthusiasm and faith in God will become contagious,

lighting a fire within yourself and inspiring others to pursue their dreams.

Set yourself achievable goals

You need to dream big, use your imagination, but set yourself achievable goals as you pursue your vision.

"If your goals are good, you will be respected." Proverbs 11:27 (GNT). If you set good, achievable goals, you will not only be respected by others but also boost your self-respect as you see them fulfilled.

When I married my lovely wife, Caroline, I told her I had a vision to become a pastor. We then set goals to make it happen. We attend a Bible college to gain knowledge and train for the ministry. After graduation, we sought every opportunity to become involved in the life of a local church while holding down secular jobs. During this time, we also pioneered a church as an outreach. I was eventually invited to join the ministry team of a large charismatic church in Melbourne, where I began as a full-time associate pastor. I was then obedient to the call to the Mission field in Papua New Guinea, where we helped establish a Bible College. On our return to Australia, I became the senior pastor of a great church.

Whatever you may be thinking at the moment, God wants to give you a future and a hope. He has a unique plan and purpose for your life.

God wants you to abound in hope

God calls Himself the God of hope and wants you to abound in hope by the power of the Holy Spirit.

"Now may the God of hope fill you with all joy and peace in believing, that you may abound in hope by the power of the Holy Spirit." Romans 15:13.

This reveals something of God's positive nature.

If we have hope and a positive outlook, it means our belief system will be filled with hope and be characterised by joy and peace as we believe in and trust God, despite outward circumstances. We can overcome the odds that seem to work against us. His hope does not leave us disappointed because He fills our hearts with the assurance of His love. *"Now hope does not disappoint, because the love of God has been poured out in our hearts by the Holy Spirit who was given to us."* Romans 5:3-5.

Hope does not disappoint. That may sound like a contradiction. As we pursue our hopes and dreams, we will inevitably face disappointments, discouragements, difficulties, detours, and delays. Nevertheless, we should never give up hope for a positive outcome, for God is faithful and will not let us down.

Robert H. Schuller, a visionary and the founder of the Crystal Cathedral in Garden Grove, California, is quoted as saying, "Let your hopes, not your hurts, shape your future." It is your choice! Schuller did not begin at the Crystal Cathedral; he started his church in a drive-in theatre, preaching from the snack bar rooftop. He went through many disappointments, but never gave up on his hopes and dreams. He went on television with the "Hour of Power," broadcasting his church to millions.

When we refuse to give up hope, it means that even when we are knocked down, we can always rise up again in Jesus' name, for as long as we have hope, we have the opportunity for success. *"For there is hope for a tree that is cut down, and it will sprout again, and that its tender shoots will not cease. Though its roots may grow old in the earth, and its stump may die in the ground, yet at the scent of water it will bud and spring forth branches like a plant."* Job 14:7-9.

There is always hope, even when all seems lost and dying; there is still hope. At the scent of water, which we can liken to the word and the Holy Spirit entering a situation that seems lifeless, life can burst forth where we thought there was none.

Faith was the substance of things hoped for. Hoping for something unseen but yet to happen. Go after your dreams, never give up.

"Now faith is the substance of things hoped for, the evidence of things not seen." Hebrews 11:1.

The things we hope for relate to the promises God has made to us in His word. This is the evidence we need for things we have not yet seen. This is the basis for our faith.

"By faith we understand that the worlds were framed by the word of God, so things which are seen are not made of things which are visible." Hebrews 11:3.

Sometimes God does unusual things to test our faith and our hopes to see if we trust Him.

The Lord told Jeremiah that his relative would approach him to offer his land for sale in Anathoth, located in the country of Benjamin, and that he was to buy it. He did not want to, because he knew the Chaldeans would occupy it. But he obeyed God and bought it. *"So, I bought the field from Hanamel, the son of my uncle who was in Anathoth."* Jeremiah 32:9.

Although Jeremiah did what he was told and bought the land, he began to reason with the Lord because it made no sense to him. He had foreseen that the land would be given to the Chaldeans, who had laid siege to Jerusalem. "And you have said to me, O Lord God, "Buy the field for money and take witnesses! – yet the city has been given to the Chaldeans." Jeremiah 32:25.

Is there anything too hard for God?

When Jeremiah began to question God, God answered Jeremiah with a rhetorical question posed by God Himself to the prophet. *"Is there anything too hard for Me?"* Jeremiah 32: 26-27. Why then would God pose such a question about Himself when the answer is obvious? God wanted Jeremiah to put his hope and trust in Him because He had promised to restore the land to Israel in the future, despite the ongoing destruction. Jeremiah probably thought he had bought a "white elephant," considering the land that he had purchased would be worthless. However, this was more of a symbolic act by God to get Jeremiah and the people to put their hope and trust in Him, so they would know He was faithful to His word and restore the land to Israel. The Lord had already promised to do this. *"Men will buy fields for money, sign deeds and seal them, and take witnesses in the land of Benjamin, in the places around Jerusalem, in the cities of Judah, in the cities of the mountains, in the cities of the lowland, and in the cities of the South: for I will cause their captivities to return, says the Lord."* Jeremiah 32:44.

We are not told what happened to the land Jeremiah actually purchased. Still, the promise of restoration tied to it was fulfilled after seventy years of exile in Babylon. The Jewish people returned to Judah, where land ownership and life eventually returned to normal. (See Ezra and Nehemiah).

The point is "nothing is too hard for God." We need to trust God, be positive, and remain filled with faith and hope for the future, despite the circumstances.

YOUR THOUGHTS SHAPE YOUR LIFE

Chapter 16

Speak positively, or stay silent

If you agree with God, speak up; if not, be quiet. Let's consider what takes place at a wedding. If you do not agree with the marriage, then you must either speak up or remain silent. The phrase "speak now or forever hold your peace" is usually a part of the traditional Christian wedding ceremony. It is a formal declaration made by the celebrant during the ceremony just before the exchange of vows. In some countries, it is a requirement to give an opportunity; if anyone knows of a legal reason why the couple should not marry, they must speak up before the marriage is solemnised. The fuller version is usually "If any person here can show just cause why these two may not be joined together in Holy matrimony – let them speak now or forever hold their peace."

I have taken the liberty of applying this as a play on words to promote a positive perspective on our attitude to our faith in the word of God. I believe God would have us speak positively about his word or hold our peace.

The example of Zacharias

I find Zacharias's encounter with the Angel Gabriel to be a good example of what I am suggesting.

> *"And when Zacharias saw him, he was troubled, and fear fell upon him. But the angel said to him, "Do not be afraid, Zacharias, for your prayer is heard; and your wife Elizabeth will bear you a son, and you shall call his name John."* Luke 1:12-13

It appears that they had been praying for a child for some time, as the angel said, "Your prayers have been heard." The angel also provided an outline of the kind of ministry and impact that their son, John, would have in his day. But Zacharias began to question how this could happen, given their advanced years. But the angel was not impressed.

> *"And Zacharias said to the angel, "How shall I know this? For I am an old man, and my wife is well advanced in years." And the angel answered and said to him, "I am Gabriel who stands in the presence of God, and was sent to speak to you and bring you these glad tidings."*

> *"But behold, you shall be mute and not able to speak until the day these things take place because you did not believe my words, which will be fulfilled in their own time."* Luke 1:18-20.

The point is, if we cannot believe the word the Lord has given us and speak positive words of faith, it is better to be mute or say nothing than to nullify it. Speak in faith now, or hold your peace.

There is a common phrase we use when we speak out

of turn or say something unwise: we use the idiom to "put one's foot in one's mouth." We realise we have said something inappropriate, offensive, or embarrassing when we did not intend to. I have made the mistake, and I know other pastors have, of praying for a woman and asking her if she was pregnant to have her say, "No, I am not." Or the time I asked a man, "Is this your mother?" He said, "No, it's my wife." That is "putting one's foot in one's mouth".

The angel Gabriel ensured that Zacharias would not make things worse by making him mute. However, when their baby was born, a dispute arose over his name; his mother said he would be called John, but the relatives argued that no one by that name was among them. When they asked Zacharias, he remained silent and asked for something to write on.

"He asked for a writing tablet, and wrote, saying, "His name is John"……..Immediately his mouth was opened, and his tongue loosed, and he spoke praising God." Luke 1:63-64.

So, once Zacharias agreed to call his name "John", which is what the angel had told him to do, he was no longer mute but was immediately able to speak again.

Mary is in complete agreement

On the other hand, when the angel appeared to Mary, he told her that she would become pregnant and bear a son. He said that this Son would be called Jesus, He would reign over the house of Jacob forever, and that his kingdom would have no end. Apart from wondering how this could be possible, seeing that she was a virgin. When she was told that the Holy Spirit would overshadow her and that her Son would be called the

Son of God. Instead of doubting and asking further questions, she replied,

"Behold, the maidservant of the Lord! Let it be to me according to your word." And the angel departed from her." Luke 1:38. She was in complete agreement!

I think it is sometimes wise for us to keep quiet until we can agree with the word of God, rather than trying to reason it away, which would make it ineffective.

The power of the spoken word

Once you agree with the word of God, it is time to speak up and declare it to be so. It is no longer time to hold your peace, especially if you are in a dry place or a battle; it is time to engage in a war of words and speak words of faith into your situation.

The prophet Ezekiel did just that when God showed him a valley full of very dry bones. And the Lord asked him if these bones can live. To which he wisely says, "O Lord, You know."

"Again, He said to me, "Prophecy to these bones and say to them, "O dry bones, hear the word of the Lord!".... "So, I prophesied as He commanded me, and breath came into them, and they lived, and stood upon their feet, and an exceeding great army." Then He said to me, "Son of man, these bones are the whole house of Israel." Ezekiel 37:3-4,10-11.

Nothing happened until Ezekiel prophesied and spoke over the very dry bones. Then came the miracle of sinews and flesh and the breath of life, causing them to come to life and stand on their feet like a mighty army. There is power in speaking a prophetic word from the Lord over a situation. If you think your preaching is to dry bones every week, do not be put off by appearances; keep believing that your words have the power to impart life to them.

Speaking the Word in faith

There was great authority in the words that Jesus and the early apostles spoke over people. A Roman army centurion came to Jesus, pleading with Him to heal his servant who was lying at home paralysed, and dreadfully tormented.

> *"And Jesus said to him, "I will come and heal him." The centurion said, "Lord, I am not worthy that You should come under my roof. But only speak a word, and my servant will be healed." For I also am a man under authority, having soldiers under me, and I say to this one, "Go", and he goes; and to another, "Come", and he comes; and to my servant "Do this", and he does it. When Jesus heard it, He marvelled and said to those who followed, "Assuredly, I say to you, I have not found such great faith, not even in Israel."* Matthew 8:8-10. This Roman centurion said, "I am a man under authority." He understood how the authority and power of the spoken word worked in the army and applied it to his sick servant. Jesus called this great faith.

Jesus preached and spoke the word with authority and power; His words healed and delivered people from all kinds of sickness and disease, and as a result, many creative miracles occurred.

Believe, before you speak

The apostle Paul believed before he spoke in faith.

This is what he said, *"Since we have the same spirit of faith, according to what is written, "I believed and therefore I spoke," we also believe and therefore speak."* 2 Corinthians 4:13.

Paul declares that he has the same spirit of faith as those in the Old Testament who, despite their difficulties, still spoke in faith, quoting from Psalm 116:10.

"For you have delivered my soul from death, my eyes from tears and my feet from falling. I will walk before the Lord in the land of the living. I believed, therefore I spoke, I am greatly afflicted."

Paul quotes this in the context of David's persecution and suffering, as he faced the possibility of death, but boldly declares his faith in God.

Paul applies this to his own life and ministry when facing the possibility of death; nothing will stop him from preaching the gospel. He believes this with all his heart. Despite facing opposition and adversity, he trusts that the Lord will deliver him and declares it in faith.

Perhaps a word of caution is appropriate. We should not be thinking that if we "Blab it, we can automatically grab it." We must believe the word in the context of the situation we are facing. I am not suggesting that our confession alone is enough to get what we want without the Holy Spirit's conviction or inspiration.

Some bold declarations spoken in faith

Jesus our Saviour and Lord – *"I am the resurrection and the life. He who believes in Me, though he may die, he shall live."* (John 11:25).

The apostle Paul – *"I am not ashamed of the gospel of Christ, for it is the power of God unto salvation for everyone who believes."* (Romans 1:16).

The apostle Peter – *"Though now you do not see him, yet believing you rejoice with joy inexpressible and full of glory, receiving the end of your faith – the salvation of your souls."* (1 Peter 1:8-9).

Reinhard Bonnke, an evangelist, especially in Africa, described his ministry as "Plundering Hell and Populating Heaven". He led thousands to Christ.

Kathryn Kuhlman – A healing ministry with signs, wonders, and miracles, famously said, "I believe in miracles with every atom of my being."

Smith Wigglesworth – A ministry of healing and boldness of faith, who even raised the dead on several occasions, would often say, "Only Believe, I'm not moved by what I see. I'm moved only by what I believe."

YOUR THOUGHTS SHAPE YOUR LIFE

Chapter 17

You need to recharge your spirit

We live in a world where many of our essential devices, such as smartphones, laptops, computers, medical equipment, and electric vehicles, require recharging. To do this, we must plug them into the necessary power source: an electrical outlet for recharging.

If we do not recharge them, their batteries will run out of power, may corrode, and become inefficient or unusable. To keep them working, we must continually recharge them.

It is a bit like that for us as Christians; we need to take time out of our busy schedules to recharge our spirit and mind by connecting with the Lord, who is our source of energy.

Moses said, "I will turn aside"

Moses was tending his father-in-law's flock at Mount Horeb when he saw a bush burning, but the flames did not consume it, so he turned aside to see it.

"Then Moses said, I will now turn aside and see this great sight, why the bush does not burn." So, when the Lord saw that he turned aside to look, God called to him from the midst of the bush and said, "Moses, Moses!" And he said, "Here I am." Exodus 3:3-4.

God used the burning bush to get Moses to turn aside to investigate what was happening. The point is, are we willing to turn aside from our busy lifestyle to spend time with no one greater than Jesus?

It was at the burning bush that God spoke to Moses and revealed to him that He was the God of his father, as well as the God of Abraham, Isaac, and Jacob. God also revealed that He had heard the cry of His people who were oppressed by slavery in Egypt and that He would send Moses to Pharaoh to lead the children of Israel out of Egypt. You might be saying, "Well, God is not calling me like He did Moses." That may be so, but He still expects us to set aside our business and pray, meditate on the Word, and fellowship with Him. During these times, our spiritual batteries are recharged, and we receive fresh inspiration and direction from the Lord, enabling us to refresh our faith and maintain a positive outlook.

How to avoid burnout in a busy world

We need to be mindful of our priorities. In a busy world, burnout often stems from saying yes to too many things. We need to clarify our values, along with our vision and purpose, to identify what is important to us: faith, family, health, friends, rest, and relaxation. We need to learn to say no to unnecessary things that may burden us. We need to step back from draining relationships or specific commitments that demand our time and energy. We can fall into the trap of depleting our energy on them.

The primary thing we need to do to avoid burnout is to stay connected to our source of life. Jesus assured us that we can do nothing by our own effort alone; we need to abide in Him if we are to be fruitful.

"Abide in Me and I in you. As the branch cannot bear fruit of itself, unless it abides in the vine, neither can you unless you abide in Me. I am the Vine, you are the branches. He who abides in me and I in him, bears much fruit; for without Me you can do nothing." John 15:4-5. Just as branches need sap —the source of life —from the vine to bear fruit, we also need to tap into Jesus.

Even Jesus said, *"I can do nothing of myself." "Most assuredly, I say to you, the Son can do nothing of Himself, but what He sees the Father do; for whatever He does, the Son also does in like manner."* John 5:19.

Jesus spent a lot of time in prayer

Jesus often withdrew to pray alone. *"Now in the morning, having risen a long while before daylight, He went out and departed to a solitary place; and there He prayed. And Simon and those who were with Him searched for Him. When they found Him, they said to Him, "Everyone is looking for you."* Mark 1:35-36.

I find this verse challenging for two reasons. *Firstly*, Jesus went out to pray early in the morning. I find this is a good habit to get into. If we start the day by drawing aside to pray and have our devotions, it seems to recharge us and prepare us for the rest of the day.

Secondly, when the disciples found Him, they said, "Everyone is looking for you." He could have become so caught up in the demands of ministry that he might have missed prayer, saying, "I am too busy to pray." How many of you have done that? I know I have, but you cannot keep it up for long before you begin to burn out. There is nothing worse than a flat spiritual battery; you can make a lot of noise but accomplish nothing worthwhile.

It was not just early mornings; on occasion, Jesus prayed all night. *"Now it came to pass in those days that he went out to the mountain to pray, and continued all night in prayer to God."* Luke 6:12. The next day, He chose twelve of His disciples and named them as apostles.

"I have so much to do that I shall spend the first three hours in prayer." Martin Luther responded with this in answer to the question about his plans for the day.

Just a word of caution: I think we need to be careful not to turn our prayer time into a religious ritual; instead, let the Holy Spirit lead us.

I remember staying in a pastor's house as the visiting speaker for his church. He insisted that I join him for prayer at 4 a.m. each morning. He was working his way through the "Lord's Prayer." His heart was in the right place, but morning after morning, it felt more like a religious ritual than a joyous time of prayer led by the Holy Spirit and waiting on the Lord. I remember the days seemed long, and we seemed tired rather than refreshed.

During my time on the mission field in Papua New Guinea, I felt compelled to pray and fast. Although it wasn't my intention, I ended up praying and fasting for forty days. It was an experience I share in my book "Hungry for God." Although it was a great experience, I concluded that we are under grace and you do not have to pray and fast to hear from God, but it certainly helps in times of need.

The clock and the compass keep us busy

Are we making time to pray? We have our battles between the clock and the compass. The clock tells us we have demands upon our time, and it is limited. The compass tells us we have a specific direction, purpose, and vision to pursue, and we need to stay on course and avoid distractions.

This is an ongoing struggle for Christians today, in our busy world with all its demands. It is a matter of sorting out our priorities. I would suggest that prayer is a top priority.

I am the first to admit that this is an ongoing battle for me. But not for Jesus! Jesus seemed to strike a balance between the clock and the compass in His private prayer time and public ministry.

"However, the report went around concerning Him all the more; and great multitudes came together to hear, and to be healed by Him of their infirmities. So, He Himself would often withdraw into the wilderness and pray." Luke 5:15-16. Jesus withdrew and prayed regularly.

The early church prayed together

The church was in prayer when God poured out His Holy

Spirit on the day of Pentecost (Acts 1:14), and we see the church continuing to pray together throughout the book of Acts. Although individuals would spend time in prayer, it was noticeable how often the church prayed together as a group. *"And they continued steadfastly in the apostle's doctrine and fellowship, in the breaking of bread (communion) and in prayers."* Acts 2:42.

This is the way the early church prayed when they began to face opposition. *"Now, Lord, look on their threats, and grant to Your servants that with all boldness they may speak Your word, by stretching out Your hand to heal, and that signs and wonders may be done through the name of Your holy Servant Jesus."* Acts 4:29-30. Although they were threatened with persecution for keeping quiet and not preaching the gospel, they prayed for boldness to continue speaking the Word of God.

When I was pastoring in Lismore, we would occasionally hold all-night prayer meetings in the church. We had a makeshift roster, with people coming for whatever time they could give or staying as long as they liked. They were long and laborious nights for some. However, God knew the intention of our hearts, and as a result, I believe the church and Christian School have prospered over the years, reaping the benefits of those prayers.

Taking time out to refresh your spirit today

We read in Acts 3:19, "times of refreshing come from the presence of the Lord." So, I would encourage you to engage in prayer and other activities that bring you into the conscious presence of the Lord. Here are some suggestions to help Christians refresh and recharge their spiritual batteries.

1. By prayer and meditating on the word.
2. By attending retreats and conferences.
3. By attending the church's worship services.
4. By attending teaching seminars.
5. By watching videos and reading books.

Whatever you do, make sure you are continually filled with the Holy Spirit. *"Do not be drunk with wine, in which is dissipation; but be filled with the Spirit, speaking to one another in psalms and hymns and spiritual songs, singing and making melody in your heart to the Lord, giving thanks always for all things to God the Father in the Name of our Lord Jesus Christ, submitting to one another in the fear of God."* Ephesians 5:18-21. Sounds like a church service you would want to be involved in!

The primary objective of taking time out to recharge your spirit and refresh your mind is to be filled with the Holy Spirit, to have a fire in your belly, to be positive, optimistic, and filled with hope and faith, believing that all things are possible with God.

YOUR THOUGHTS SHAPE YOUR LIFE

Chapter 18

Joyful faith, fun, and fellowship

We are building on the previous chapter, which emphasised recharging and refreshing your spiritual batteries through prayer and your relationship with God.

A part of that process, from a Christian perspective, is the lighter side of recharging our batteries: embracing joyful faith, fun, and fellowship. I have observed that most successful individuals and churches seek opportunities to do this through various activities.

Although we do not have direct references, we can infer that this lifestyle was integral to Jesus and his disciples' lives and continued in the early churches. This would have provided them with some form of relief from the strenuous demands of their ministry.

"Then the apostles gathered together unto Jesus and told Him all things, both what they had done and what they had taught. And he said

to them, "Come aside by yourselves to a deserted place and rest a while." Matthew 6:31. I should have imagined that there would be plenty of joyful fun as they drew aside and rested, eating together, sharing fellowship, and building faith as they did so.

Making allowances today

I think you will agree with me that there is excellent value in having fellowship over a cup of coffee, whether it's at a Coffee shop, in a home, or at church. It provides the opportunity to develop relationships by interacting with people as you share life.

Most churches, aside from Sunday meetings, offer other programs or events that provide opportunities for community building during these times. These include home groups, church camps, conferences, sporting events, picnics, soup kitchens, op shops, Christian schooling, religious instruction in secular schools, chaplaincies in various organisations, and so on.

I recall when I started in full-time ministry in Melbourne; we had a home group that met regularly in our home. It was a fantastic group of people, filled with fun, laughter, and Bible studies. We would often do fun things together. I was reminiscing, looking at photos of a day trip from Melbourne to the nearest snow, where we had a great time tobogganing down the slopes together. Even though we are separated by geography, I feel we have a bond with those people that will last forever.

On the mission field in Papua New Guinea, we had lots of fun. The college students balanced their studies by regularly playing table tennis, basketball, and soccer. Some of us would pile into our old Dyna bus and head off to a secluded beach. As elders and leaders, we would often spend time together praying and discussing our vision for the college and church.

Upon returning to Australia and being appointed senior pastor in Lismore, where we stayed for twenty-one years, we met regularly as elders. The church fielded cricket and touch football teams, as well as groups involved in golf, netball, tennis, music, and other activities. Being much younger myself, I remember some battles on the tennis court with my associate pastor, Rod Dymock (Foreword for this book), who, being 6'.4" (193cm), was so hard to beat.

When I retired, I handed the church and Christian School over to Rod and his wife, Margaret, who, together with their family, took the church and school to another level before passing them both on to Dave and Bernie Winter, who continue to do a great work. We all need a balanced life that blends faith, moments of joy, and meaningful, loving relationships, which, in turn, cause us to rejoice and be positive regardless of our circumstances.

Jesus was full of joy (Luke 10:21). Jesus went to weddings and ate with sinners and friends. He mixed with all kinds of people, made time for children, and sometimes told stories with subtle humour. We can only assume that He and his disciples were filled with joy.

What about a good dose of laughter?

There is nothing like a good sense of humour to lighten the burdens and pressures we grapple with daily. As ministers, we continually encounter serious situations. People are seeking help and ministry for all kinds of complex issues, where they are trying to deal with stress, abuse, grief, that need delicate and serious attention. I am not suggesting that these people need a good dose of laughter while going through their trials and troubles. Perhaps that will come later, once they work their way through these difficulties. In the meantime, we need to be sensitive to their needs. The Bible declares there is "A time to weep, and a time to laugh, a time to mourn and a time to dance. Ecclesiastes 3:4.

Charles R. Swindoll, in his book *Laugh Again*, says, "It is certain that our circumstances are not the things that make us joyful. If we wait for them to get just right, we will never laugh again." Charles has a section in his book discussing the value of friends with a good sense of humour and how having fun with them keeps him sane. "I cannot imagine where I would be today were it not for that handful of friends and family who have given me a heart of joy. Let's face it, friends and family make life a lot more fun."

I thank God for my wife, family, and friends who have a good sense of humour. There have been times when my youngest daughter, Sharon, and I have burst into fits of laughter, even when we're trying to be serious. It is somewhat of a release valve for tension and anxiety.

When I was pastoring in Lismore, my associate Rod Dymock had a great, subtle sense of humour. We would often burst into laughter when meeting in my office, much to the embarrassment of the office staff. Once again, I think it was a release from the serious issues and pressure of the ministry.

Laughter is not just for releasing tension. It is something we do when we celebrate an exciting event or a victory. Because it gives us great joy, we usually fill the atmosphere with laughter as we celebrate.

The children of Israel celebrated their release from captivity with joy, laughter, and singing.

"When the Lord brought back the captivity of Zion, we were like those who dream. Then our mouth was filled with laughter, and our tongue with singing" (Psalm 126).

The bible implies that a good dose of cheerfulness (laughter) is as good as medicine for a broken or disheartened spirit. *"A merry (cheerful) heart does good like a medicine, but a broken spirit dries the bones."* Psalm 17:22.

Cheerful (hilarious) giving

"So let each one give as he purposes in his heart, not grudgingly or of necessity; for God loves a cheerful giver." 2 Corinthians 9:7.

The word cheerful in Greek is hilaros, from which we get our English word hilarious. In this context, it means to be prompted to do something with a joyful heart. The original English use of the word hilarious refers to something we find extremely funny. It is not that we see giving to be extremely funny, but God is challenging our attitude because He knows how hard it is for most people to give with a cheerful heart. The broader context of this verse emphasises the benefits of generosity over stinginess, highlighting the principle that what you sow is what you will reap. If you sow bountifully, you will reap bountifully, or if you sow sparingly, you will reap sparingly.

Do not let religion rob you of your joy

Some religious Christians look as though they have been baptised in lemon juice. They tend to be legalistic, appearing hard and lacking joy, showing little love and grace, and being ever ready to defend what they believe to be right. I know some have been taught to be sober to appear holy and pious, confusing reverence with rigidity and religious practices.

I recently spoke with a woman who attends an Orthodox church about the format of church services. She was telling me how they follow a solemn religious liturgy to worship God. I can understand that, and if that is their preferred way of worship, so be it.

When I told her our services were filled with joy and singing, accompanied by clapping or raised hands in worship, she was surprised. She indicated that if she acted that way in her church, it would not be acceptable and that she would be asked to leave.

I believe we must be cautious not to return to a legalistic religious system of any kind, such as the law that Jesus came to liberate us from. A dispute arose in the early church over what was considered clean or unclean to eat and drink under the law. Paul addressed the issue by letting them know they were no longer walking in love while they were fighting over this issue and reminded them that *"The kingdom of God is not eating and drinking, but righteousness, and peace, and joy in the Holy Spirit."* Romans 14:17.

Joy is a spiritual quality imparted by the Holy Spirit regardless of our circumstances. It sustains us through difficult times and gives us the strength to endure hardships in times of sorrow.

"Do not sorrow, for the joy of the Lord is your strength." Nehemiah 8:10. The joy of the Lord can bring strength to our spirit, mind and body.

The point is that joyful faith, fun, and fellowship go hand in hand to help us develop a belief system that inspires positive attitudes and leads to a healthier lifestyle.

YOUR THOUGHTS SHAPE YOUR LIFE

Chapter 19

Take time to think outside the box

The phrase "think outside the box" originated from a classic puzzle involving nine dots arranged in a 3x3 grid. The challenge is to connect all nine dots using four straight lines, without lifting the pen from the paper and without retracing any line. Most people stay within the perceived square. The key to solving it is to extend the lines beyond that imaginary square, hence "to think outside the box."

The phrase gained popularity and is often used to motivate people across various fields to become more inventive by thinking beyond the norm. Most of us are constrained by our self-imposed boundaries (the box) and must take time to think outside them to be creative and achieve something new and extraordinary.

In the movie *Dead Poets Society*, John Keating, played by Robin Williams, is an unorthodox English teacher at a conservative all-boys preparatory school.

There is a scene where he gathers his students around a trophy case filled with photos of alumni and tells them to look at the faces of those who came before them. He explains that these men were once in their position – young and full of potential - but are now fertilising daffodils. He encourages them to live life to the fullest and make their lives extraordinary. He then delivers the Latin phrase "Carpe diem." "Seize the day, boys." "Make your lives extraordinary." He says it to inspire students to think outside the box.

Martin Luther, German theologian, professor, pastor, and church reformer, seized the opportunity to think outside the box of the Catholic system and nailed his ninety-five theses to the church door in Wittenberg in 1517, attacking the church's sale of indulgences. This led to the Protestant Reformation, which proclaimed, "The just shall live by faith," changing the course of Christianity.

William Wilberforce thought outside the box and seized the opportunity as a politician with an evangelical Christian background to campaign against slavery. This ultimately led to its abolition in the British Empire. This formed what was commonly referred to as the Anti-Slavery Society. There are many other turning points in history we could mention, but let's consider the spiritual implications.

Allowing for the wonder of the Holy Spirit

The Holy Spirit is not confined to human traditions and strategies. He often disrupts the norm and leads us to do wondrous and creative things 'outside the box' to advance the kingdom of God.

Rod Dreher, in his book *Living in Wonder: Finding Mystery and Meaning in a Secular Age*, argues that most of Western culture has become 'disenchanted' – citing a loss of belief in or openness to the supernatural power of the Holy Spirit. We are more focused on a set of doctrinal boxes we must tick, but in doing so, we leave a desperate void for a sense of enchantment through the wonder of the Holy Spirit's creative power. A classic biblical example is when the apostle Peter was asked to preach the gospel to the household of Cornelius (Acts 10). At first, he resisted on the premise that traditionally, the Jews avoided close contact with the Gentiles. He reluctantly went, and the Holy Spirit broke through cultural and religious barriers, falling on the Gentiles while Peter was sharing the gospel, even before they were baptised in water.

Those who thought outside the box

There are numerous biblical examples of people guided by God to think outside the box and act in faith, achieving remarkable accomplishments. I will briefly mention a few individuals whom God inspired to think differently, act in faith, and accomplish amazing feats.

Noah built an Ark in faith, far from water, on dry land, expecting a flood that would cover the earth.

Moses raised his staff over the Red Sea, causing it to part and allowing the children of Israel to escape from the Egyptians.

David, who faced the giant Goliath and brought him down with a slingshot, giving Israel victory.

Joshua and his army marched around Jericho seven times

on the seventh day, blowing trumpets, and all the people shouted until the walls of the city collapsed.

Jesus fed over 5000 with two fish and five loaves of bread, then took up twelve baskets full of leftovers.

Peter, when he saw Jesus who was walking on water, stepped out of the boat and walked on water when Jesus told him to come to Him.

Peter and John, when they saw a man who was lame asking for alms, said to him, "Silver and gold we do not have, but we give you what we do have, in the name of Jesus Christ of Nazareth, rise up and walk." They lifted him up, and his ankle bones received strength, and he was healed.

Paul and Silas were singing and praising God in a dark and gloomy prison at midnight. When God responded with a sudden earthquake, the prison doors opened, their chains fell off, and they were set free.

As Christians, we have God-given opportunities to think outside the box and do extraordinary things. But do we recognise those opportunities and seize them when we have the chance? When God opens a door for us, we sometimes only get one chance to seize the opportunity, and then it disappears, perhaps never to present itself again. I think that when we near the end of our lives, we will either look back in regret and say, "If only I had," or say, with contentment, "I thank God, I seized that opportunity, stepped out in faith, to make it happen."

Making the most of an unlikely opportunity

The biblical story of the four starving lepers is an inspiring tale of men in a hopeless situation facing certain death, who were prepared to think outside the box, seize an unlikely opportunity, and save themselves and a city.

> *"Now there were four leprous men at the entrance of the gate; and they said to one another, "Why are we sitting here until we die?" If we say, "We will enter the city, the famine is in the city, and we shall die there. And if we sit here, we shall die also. Now therefore, come let us surrender to the army of the Syrians. If they keep us alive, we shall live, and if they kill us, we shall only die."* 2 Kings 7:3-4. They had nothing to lose; they were thinking outside the box by going to the enemy camp.

When the four starving lepers entered the camp, to their surprise, no one was there. The Lord had caused the enemy to hear the sound of a mighty army marching toward them, and they had fled for their lives. They had left behind plenty of food, drink, livestock and supplies.

After they had fed themselves, they said to one another, *"We are not doing right. This day is a day of good news, and we remain silent. If we wait till morning light, some punishment will come upon us."* 2Kings 7:9.

When they returned to the city and spread the good news, the people who had been starving in the city due to the siege rushed out to the enemy camp and helped themselves to the food. So, because four lepers were prepared to step outside the box and seize what opportunity they had, the whole city was saved.

When God opens a door, seize the opportunity

When God opens a door for us, we must seize the opportunity while the door is still open. We need to think positively and put our faith into action. When God called us to the mission field in Papua New Guinea, He opened the door for us in a fantastic way. Although we were stepping into the unknown, we were confident that God was with us. However, we had to think outside our comfort zone. Leaving behind a new house we had just built in Melbourne, a great church, our parents, family, and friends, to go to a foreign country, we went in faith. As a result, many lives were saved and changed.

When we returned to Australia, some six years later, God opened the door for us to move to Lismore, where I served as the senior pastor of the church (Centre Church) and chairman of the Christian school board (Summerland Christian College) for the next twenty-one years.

We read how God opened the door for the apostles and the early church to preach the gospel on several occasions, but left it up to them to seize the opportunity by faith. The Holy Spirit gave them power far beyond their natural abilities, enabling them to accomplish great things, with God confirming the word they preached with signs, wonders, and miracles.

This boldness, empowered by the Holy Spirit, spread and caused the apostles and believers to seize every opportunity to share the gospel. It was the catalyst God used to open doors for rapid church growth.

Paul was very aware of God opening and closing doors for the gospel. *"But I will tarry in Ephesus until Pentecost. A great and effective door has opened to me, and there are many adversaries."* 1 Corinthians 16:8-9. We need to note that although God had opened a door for Paul, he was well aware of the adversities he would still have to face.

The early church would pray for God to open doors so that they could share the gospel. *"Continue earnestly in prayer, be vigilant in it with thanksgiving; meanwhile, praying also for us, that God would open to us a door for the word, to speak the mystery of Christ."* Colossians 4:3.

I believe churches should pray that God will open doors for them to present the gospel in innovative ways within their community.

As an individual or as a church, be led by the Holy Spirit. Here is a list of practical considerations that might help you to think outside the box.

1. *Challenge your traditions* – Ask: "Why do we always do things this way?" "What are some alternatives?"

2. *Reframe the way you think* – Ask: "How can we make this more relevant?" "Are we addressing issues people are interested in?"

3. *Brainstorm in groups* – Consider a wide range of ideas, even if they seem silly. Out of quantity comes quality.

4. *Think big possibilities* – Ask: "What if money were not a problem?" "What can we do with what we have?"

5. *Experiment wisely* – Test ideas in a small way to create clarity, and enlarge on them.

YOUR THOUGHTS SHAPE YOUR LIFE

Do not leave it all to the church; seize every opportunity to think outside the box, and you will be surprised at what God can do through you.

Chapter 20

Are you thinking beyond the grave?

The reality is that human life is frail and limited compared to the eternal life that lies beyond the grave. I do not want to sound morbid, but the reality is that nobody escapes their appointment with death.

"What man can live and not see death? Can he deliver his life from the power of the grave?" Psalm 89:48.

It never ceases to amaze me that, although death is the one certainty in life that we all face, very few people give serious thought to preparing for what may lie beyond the grave. We need to ask questions like "What have I done with my life?" "How will I be remembered?" "Do I have much time left?" "Is there any hope of life beyond the grave?" "What should I do about my faith in God?"

I'm referring to what awaits you in the afterlife. Where are you going to spend eternity in heaven or in hell? I have had people try to convince me that there is nothing after death. They believe that we no longer exist. I have tried to convince them otherwise, hoping they will remember to change their minds in their final moments on earth. Besides, they have nothing to lose and everything to gain if eternal life is a reality, which I am convinced it is, based on my faith in the word of God.

I recently came across a fictitious analogy used to understand the possible mystery we face beyond the grave. Two unborn babies were discussing what happens after delivery. One said, "Nothing, we have life now, but once we are out of this womb and detached from this umbilical cord, we die; there is nothing more." The other one said, "I think after delivery, we may take on another form of life and enter a new environment where we are free from the restrictions of this womb and can enjoy a much better life." Which one was right? I hope this is a good analogy to help you consider the possibilities of life after death.

After we die, the Bible declares that our spirits live on and return to God. *"Then the dust will return to the earth as it was, and the spirit will return to God who gave it."* Ecclesiastes 12:7.

God will determine where we spend eternity based on the decisions we make before we die.

You can spend a lifetime working on being positive and optimistic, but that alone will not help you prepare for eternity. After all, if you live to be seventy or eighty plus, what is that compared to eternity? Besides, you never know when you might die. When you do, it will be too late to start thinking about it then. *"You do not know what will happen tomorrow. For what is your life? It is even a vapour that appears for a little time and then vanishes away."* James 4:14. I was talking to a lady recently who told me she no longer attends church. When I encouraged her to go, she said, "I'll go and sort things out with God when I am good and ready." That is a risky game to play because we just read, *"You do not know what will happen tomorrow."* Please do not put it off. Now is the time to prepare for your eternal destination.

Jesus said, *"What does it profit a man if he gains the whole world, and loses his own soul? Or what will a man give in exchange for his soul?"* Mark 8:36-37.

You can spend all your time on earth striving for success, gaining riches, yet neglect the most valuable thing you have, your eternal soul. The state of your soul will determine your final eternal destination.

Encouraged by near-death experiences (NDEs)

There are many recorded accounts of Near-Death Experiences where people have clinically died, and their spirit has seen heaven, sometimes hell, and then they have been sent back and returned to their body again to tell some incredible stories. Some have written books or recorded their experiences to share with us.

Mary C. Neal, MD – Orthopaedic Surgeon, while kayaking in Chile, drowned. She says she experienced leaving her body and travelling to heaven, where she saw a lush, vibrant landscape filled with light and love, and a deep sense of peace, joy, and belonging. But she was told it wasn't her time yet and was sent back. She wrote the book *"To Heaven and Back."*

Don Piper, A Baptist minister, died in a car crash and was dead for 90 minutes. He saw a beautiful gate and a city of intense light, filled with music, colours, and sounds that don't exist on earth. He was greeted with joy by deceased friends and family.

He had a sense of perfect peace and no desire to return until he was revived. He wrote the book *"90 Minutes in Heaven."*

Colton Burpo – a four-year-old boy who, during emergency surgery, claimed he went to heaven and met Jesus, with marks in his hands and feet (scars), angels, and a miscarried sister his parents had never told him about. His story is told in the book *"Heaven Is for Real,"* which was also made into a movie.

Why choose Christianity over other religions?

The resurrection of Jesus authenticates everything He claimed to be. His resurrection is unique among the founders of other major religions.

Jesus Christ, the founder of Christianity, rose from the dead; the tomb is empty. He is alive forevermore. *Muhammad*, the founder of Islam, was buried in Medina, Saudi Arabia. *Buddha*, the founder of Buddhism, died in the 5th Century BCE. *Confucius*, the founder of Confucianism, died and was buried in China. *Moses*, the founder of Judaism, died and was buried (location unknown). *Joseph Smith*, founder of Mormonism, died and was buried in Illinois, USA. Jesus is the only one who rose from the dead and promises to resurrect you.

People fear death, usually because they think they will no longer exist and be separated from loved ones forever. But when you die, you do not cease to exist. You transition to another form of life. For believers, in a way, eternal life has already started.

Jesus said, *"I am the resurrection and the life. He who believes in Me, though he may die, he shall live. And whoever lives and believes in Me shall never die. Do you believe this?"* John 11:25-26.

"He who believes in Me shall never die." The question Jesus

asks is, "Do you believe this?" This is the challenge you are presented with: Do you believe? It's up to you to decide. Do not listen to friends and family who try to discourage you from choosing to follow Christ. I had an uncle who persisted in telling me that Christianity was a lot of rubbish.

Preparing for eternity should be your priority

Some people think preparing to die is to make sure they have made out a will for their loved ones to have an inheritance. As important as that may be, our souls must be prepared for eternity. The apostle Paul says that if you do not prepare for eternity, you are foolish and to be pitied because you have no hope for an eternal future. He tells us how crucial it is to believe in Christ, His resurrection and the resurrection of all believers before you die (1 Corinthians 15).

We are all in the same boat; there are no exceptions unless we turn to Christ. *"For the wages of sin is death, but the gift of God is eternal life in Christ Jesus our Lord."* Romans 6:23. Salvation is a gift from God to be received by faith. It is something we neither deserve nor can earn by our own merit. *"For by grace you have been saved through faith, and that not of yourselves, is the gift of God, not of works lest anyone should boast."* Ephesians 2:8-9. You may be able to boast about your good works and have a positive mindset, but as commendable as that may be, it is not the criterion for salvation.

Some years ago, I was involved in a church survey programme. We went from door to door, taking a survey to gauge people's thoughts about God and the church. The last question on the survey was, "If you were to die tonight and stand before God, and He said to you, "Why should I let you into heaven?" "What would you say?" Nine out of ten said, "Because I have lived a good life." Most people think you have to earn your way to heaven. However, the scripture is unequivocal: salvation is a gift by the grace of God, to be received by faith in Christ.

Douglas Coupland, in his book *Life after God*, does not claim to be a Christian, but he ends the book with an interesting scenario. He says he has a secret he wants to share. He leads you to a quiet place in the forest. Then he writes: "My secret is…I need God, I am sick and can no longer make it alone. I need God to help me give, because I no longer seem capable of giving, to help me be kind, as I no longer seem capable of kindness; to help me love, as I am beyond being able to love." Maybe we all feel this way at times. But I encourage you to do something about it; you do need Christ. It is no secret that Christ died for you to help you through life and prepare you for eternity.

If you are not a Christian, "repentance" means changing your mind and your direction in life. It is time for you to start thinking beyond the grave as to what your eternal destination will look like. Where are you headed, heaven or hell? There is no other alternative. It doesn't matter what your friends think or what they say you should believe about God. Make up your own mind.

The early church preached repentance. *"Repent therefore and be converted, that your sins may be blotted out, so that times of refreshing may come from the presence of the Lord."* Acts 3:19.

What are you thinking? What is your heart telling you to do? As a man thinks in his heart, so is he. You need to repent and turn to Christ for forgiveness, and you will be born again, starting a new life.

I will help you take the first step toward becoming a Christian. Say this prayer: "Lord Jesus, come into my heart and life right now. I repent of my sins and ask for your forgiveness. Please make me a new person. I confess you to be my Saviour and Lord." Thank you. Now, I would advise you to find a good church and start attending it.

If you just prayed that prayer, you may not feel any different and wonder, "How can I be sure I am saved?" Salvation is not based on your feelings; it is based on putting your faith in the written Word of God and believing what the Bible says.

"These things I have written to you who believe in the name of the Son of God, that you may know that you have eternal life, and that you may continue to believe in the name of the Son of God." 1 John 5:13.

"These things I have written to you, that you may know that you have eternal life." Our faith is grounded in the written word of God, not in our emotions or feelings; it is a deliberate decision we have made. However, change will come—if not immediately, then over time—as you continue to follow Christ.

Thank you for reading this book, and I pray it will inspire you to develop the power of positive thinking from a Christian perspective.

www.ingramcontent.com/pod-product-compliance
Lightning Source LLC
Chambersburg PA
CBHW021106080526
44587CB00010B/404